HEROES
OF
JEWISH
THOUGHT

HEROES
OF
JEWISH
THOUGHT

DEBORAH KARP

KTAV PUBLISHING HOUSE, INC.

Library of Congress Card Catalog No. 65-21743
Manufactured in the United States of America

TABLE OF CONTENTS

To my father
Rabbi Abraham Burstein
who introduced me to these
Heroes of Jewish Thought
and has striven heroically
to follow their teachings

PHOTOGRAPH CREDITS

ACKNOWLEDGMENTS

For the facts and attitudes reflected in this book, I am indebted to numerous scholars and teachers, writers and historians, among whom I must specify my parents and my instructors at the Seminary College of Jewish Studies. For valuable editorial direction throughout, I am grateful to Eli Grad. For his advice and encouragement, I owe thanks to Rabbi Abraham Ezra Millgram.

Without the continued patient guidance and counsel of my husband, Rabbi Abraham J. Karp, this book would never have taken form.

WHY THIS BOOK IS FOR YOU

This is a book about some great men whom you ought to know.

You have heard of some of them before. In this book you can get to know them better. Others you will meet for the first time.

They are worth knowing because they were all heroes, heroes of the soul and heroes of thought. Their lives show courage and strength, love of their people, loyalty to their beliefs, and faith in the justice of God.

There is a special reason for you to meet these men. They are all members of your family!

You like to hear about your own relatives, of course. You are proud when your father or uncle or cousin does something important.

When you read about Jewish heroes of the past, you are really reading about your own family. They are ancestors of yours, grandparents of your grandparents, as far back as you can trace them.

Have you been lucky enough to know your great-grandfather or great-grandmother? You would have to stay "great" more than a hundred times to come to the great-great-grandfather who was Abraham, the first Hebrew. It was 3,500 years ago that Abraham left his home to go to the land of Canaan, there to worship the one God and obey His laws.

SOME OF YOUR ANCESTORS

Abraham, Isaac and Jacob were your ancestors. They are called the fathers of the Jewish people.

The twelve sons of Jacob were the fathers of the twelve tribes of Israel. You may be of the tribe of Judah or of Levi.

Moses, who led the children of Israel out of Egypt and taught them the Torah, was in your family.

So was Joshua, who led them into the Promised Land of Canaan; and so were the judges, like Samson and Deborah; the kings, like Saul and David; and Solomon, who built the Temple in Jerusalem; the prophets, like Elijah and Amos and Isaiah; and Jeremiah and Ezekiel, who comforted the people when the Temple was destroyed.

So were Ezra and Nehemiah, who helped build a Second Temple and create a second state when the Jews were allowed to return to Jerusalem.

We can read about these ancestors of yours in the Bible. The whole world knows of their deeds and words.

AFTER THE BIBLE

On Hanukkah we read about the Maccabees who saved the Second Temple from the Greek soldiers who used it for the worship of idols.

The Maccabees were in your family too!

You have heard of other brave men who kept the Jewish people alive.

Hillel, who was strong in patience and in love of learning.

Johanan ben Zakkai, who started a school for the study of the Torah, after the Romans destroyed the Second Temple.

Akiva, who fought for the Torah and died for it. Bar Kochba his friend, the general who fought against the powerful Romans.

Judah Ha-Nasi, teacher and prince of his people.

Soldiers and fighters, wise men and kings, holy men and prophets, were among your ancestors.

Some day, when you visit Israel (which used to be called Palestine, or in Roman times, Judea, and before that, Canaan), you will find the places where these great leaders lived. You will be able to walk where they walked. Then they will seem more real to you. You will feel close to them, as you do to your own family.

OUTSIDE THE LAND OF ISRAEL

But not all of your ancestors lived in Palestine, the land of Israel. Most of the men you will meet in this book lived outside the Land of Israel. Some lived in Babylonia or in Egypt, which were near Palestine. Others lived in countries further away, in Spain and in France, in Germany and in Poland.

Why did the Jews leave their beloved Holy Land?

When the Babylonians destroyed the First Temple, they made the Jews leave their homes and go into exile in Babylonia.

When the Jews were allowed to return to build the Second Temple, a large number went back. There were many, however, who remained in exile and sent help to their brothers in the Land of Israel.

The Jews were not left alone to rule themselves and live in peace in the days of the Second Temple. Alexander the Great conquered them. After his death, kings of Syria and of Egypt tried to gain control of the land. Finally the Romans ruled.

The saddest time came when the Romans destroyed the Temple, in the year 70. Jerusalem was in ruins. Many, many Jews were sent into exile.

The brave Jews of Palestine did not give up. They rebelled against the Romans. But they could not win against the mightiest empire in the world.

Life in Palestine became harder. Jews were not allowed to live in their holy city of Jerusalem. They could not do what they wanted, and they had to pay heavy taxes to Rome.

Although Jews everywhere still loved their Holy Land, they learned to live in the many countries where they had settled.

THE PEOPLE LIVES ON

Why didn't the Jews, scattered all over the world, without a king or a land of their own, forget who they were and become like the nations around them?

There were many things to keep this people alive. There was their love of one God, their memory of the past, their study of the Torah. They never forgot the land and the language of their forefathers.

Great rabbis like Hillel and Akiva taught the people how to keep the laws of the Torah. Rabbi Judah Ha-Nasi collected the teachings of the rabbis, so that Jews all over the world might read and know them.

Later there were more explanations and more writings. This book will tell you about some of them.

HOW YOUR ANCESTORS HELPED YOU

You would have to say "great" about sixty times to see what kind of great-grandfather Hillel was to you. That would take us back to the time this book begins.

Even if you are not exactly a great-grandchild of Hillel, he can be considered an ancestor of yours. If he had not lived, you would be a different kind of person today.

He and all the other Jewish heroes helped to make you the way you are.

If Moses had not led the Jewish people out of Egypt, you and your family might be slaves in Egypt to this day.

If there had been no Maccabees, you might be a pagan today, worshipping Zeus and the other false gods of Greece.

Without the work of Rashi, of Maimonides, of all the heroes in this book, you would be very different from what you are.

That is why you are invited to meet them and to learn about them.

When you know more about these famous relatives of yours, you may understand yourself better, too.

WHEN YOU ARE OLDER

When you are older, you may get to know these great men much better. You may have the wonderful experience of reading their own words, just the way they wrote them. You will study and think about their ideas and will feel as though you can talk things over with them. They will then become really a part of your family and of your life.

You may become such a good student and such a loyal Jew that you will work for your people as they did.

In your own way, you, too, may be a Jewish hero.

UNIT ONE

THE AGE OF THE TALMUD

Two thousand years ago, Rome was considered the ruler of the world. The mighty Roman Empire reached from England in the north to Egypt in the south. Roman governors, with the help of Roman soldiers, ruled the conquered nations with an iron hand. A subject people was allowed to live in peace if it paid taxes and obeyed its masters. If a nation wanted its freedom, it soon felt the might of the Roman legions.

Most of the Empire was willing to adopt Roman gods and Roman ways. The tiny country of Palestine, which the Romans called Judea, was one of the trouble spots in the Roman Empire. When Syria had ruled this country, King Antiochus had found out that the Jews would fight rather than give up their religion. The Romans found out the same thing.

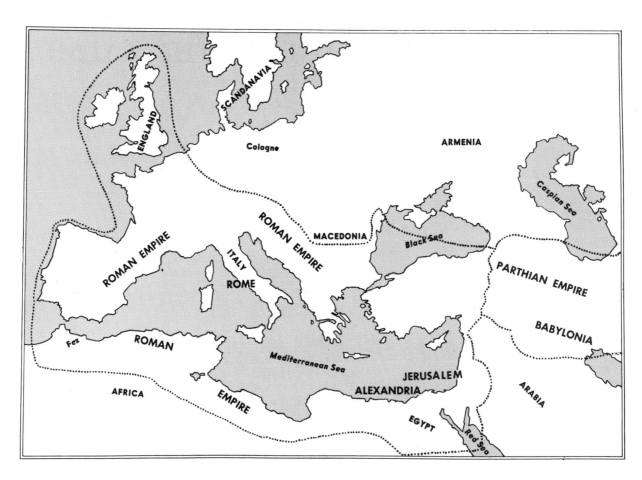

The Roman Empire ruled all the lands around the Mediterranean Sea. The Parthians ruled Babylonia to the east.

The story of Hanukkah (165 B.C.E.) reminds the Jews of the uprising of the Maccabees against Antiochus of Syria. As a result of Judah's victory, the Jews were able to worship in their Temple in Jerusalem, and to keep their religion. They were not completely free, however. Rome was beginning to take over the government of Syria and Palestine.

From the Hasmonean family, the family of Judah Maccabee, came leaders and generals

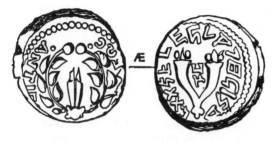

Hebrew coin struck by Antigonus Mattathias, last Hasmonean king, who ruled from 40 to 37 B.C.E.

for Palestine. Some were called kings, and there was even a queen, Alexandra. Wars were carried on, and the Kingdom of Edom was defeated and forced to become part of the Jewish people. The leaders of the Roman Empire watched and waited.

An artist's idea of the Bet Hamikdash, the Temple in Jerusalem. The large area, the Temple Mount, was surrounded by a wall.

Finally Pompey, one of the greatest of Roman conquerors, marched into Palestine (63 B.C.E.) . After invading the Temple during a service, and killing thousands of priests and worshipers, Pompey appointed a new high priest, Hyrcanus, a Jew who was friendly to Rome.

Coin struck by King Herod.

Hyrcanus and his friend Antipater, an Edomite, continued to look for favor from Rome. When the great Julius Caesar, after conquering half of Europe and fighting a civil war at home, became the powerful leader of Rome, he appointed Hyrcanus and Antipater to high positions in Judea.

After the death of Antipater, his son Herod kept the support of the Romans by giving support first to Caesar; then, after Caesar's assassination, to Brutus; then to Mark Antony, and then to Octavian. For his allegiance, Herod was appointed by Rome as king of Judea (40 B.C.E.) .

The Gentiles called him Herod the Great. The Jews called him Herod the Wicked. He built cities and rebuilt the Temple in Jerusalem, which had become old and dilapidated. His loyalty, however, was obviously to Rome, and he wanted the Jews to become more like their masters. Herod copied the Roman example in killing off his enemies. He even had his own wife and sons put to death.

The Western Wall in the Old City of Jerusalem is all that remains of the Second Temple.

Soon after Herod's death, Rome took over direct rule of Judea and the northern part of Palestine, Samaria. Procurators, stern Roman officials, tried to make the Jews keep Roman law and religion. Except for a few years when Agrippa, Herod's grandson, was allowed to rule, there was no relief from Roman oppression.

The Jews of Jerusalem rallied against the procurator Pontius Pilate when he tried to bring statues of the emperor and of pagan gods into the city. They rioted again when he tried to take money from the Temple treasury. The many small uprisings seemed ready to develop into a real rebellion against the power of Rome.

PHARISEES AND SADDUCEES

While Roman generals and legions occupied land after land, the Jews in their dominions tried to live according to the laws of their faith. The daily life of the Jew was directed by the *mitzvot,* or commandments, found in the *Torah,* or Written Law; and also the many laws and traditions which had grown up among the people and which were called the Oral, or Unwritten Law.

The Romans brought roads, courts, temples and theaters to the conquered countries; but the roads were built by forced native labor, the temples were to pagan gods, and the theaters exhibited cruel fights between gladiators and wild beasts.

As in the days of Antiochus, some Jews were attracted to the foreign civilization, and some Jewish leaders gained power through helping the invader. But also, as in the days of the Maccabees, the greatest leaders and most of the people remained faithful Jews.

The religious teachers of the Jews were called *Pharisees,* or *Perushim* in Hebrew. The rabbis and leaders who belonged to this group stressed the following of Jewish law in every detail of daily living, so that a Jew's whole life could become holy. They revered both the Written and the Oral Law. They believed that study and observance were necessary for every good Jew, and ruled that every town must have a school for children.

The *Sanhedrin,* the court of seventy-one scholars who decided questions of Jewish law, was for the most part made up of Pharisees.

Another group, the *Sadducees,* who were led by priests and by wealthier Jews, thought it important to have a strong central group in authority. They were strict in their interpretation of the Torah, emphasizing the Temple service, and not recognizing the development of the law among the people. They felt that learning and leadership belonged to the aristocrats, or leaders.

There were many who called themselves *Zealots,* who kept working with zeal towards a revolution against Rome. There were also a small number who tried to live apart in religious communities, writing and studying, and thus escape the wickedness of the world around them. These were called *Essenes.*

Ancient jars found in caves at Quram, containing some of the famous Dead Sea scrolls. These scrolls were written by a colony of scribes who were probably Essenes, living under Roman rule.

OUTSIDE THE LAND

Three million Jews lived in Palestine before the rebellion against Rome. Outside the land, there were Jews in every part of the Roman empire. Many lived in the city of Rome itself. In the great city of Alexandria in Egypt a third of the people were Jews, many of them wealthy and cultured. Here Philo the philosopher (20 B.C.E.-40 C.E.) defended

A fragment from a Dead Sea scroll, with sentences from the prophet Habakkuk. These scrolls are precious because they are the oldest manuscripts found. Some of them are over two thousand years old, and are still readable.

the Jewish religion, explaining to the pagans how the Bible and Jewish traditions taught people to be noble and virtuous.

Most of the world at this time was pagan, worshiping many gods. Pagans prayed and offered sacrifices to sun, moon, or stars; stones, trees, or rivers; and even animals. The Romans worshiped a collection of gods, beginning with Jupiter, the king; each god was supposed to have power over some part of nature. Only the Jews had the knowledge of one God. Many pagans became converts to Judaism.

The largest Jewish community outside of the Roman empire was in Babylonia, where Jews had lived for hundreds of years. When the First Temple had been destroyed (586 B.C.E.), most of the Jews had been forced to go into exile in Babylonia. Years later, when Jews were allowed to return to Jerusalem to build the Second Temple, many of the exiles remained in Babylonia. At the time when the Roman Empire was so powerful, Babylonia was ruled by the Parthians, enemies of Rome.

The Jews of Babylonia, who numbered nearly a million at this time, had more freedom than the Jews of Palestine, but still considered themselves to be in exile. All communities outside Palestine were called

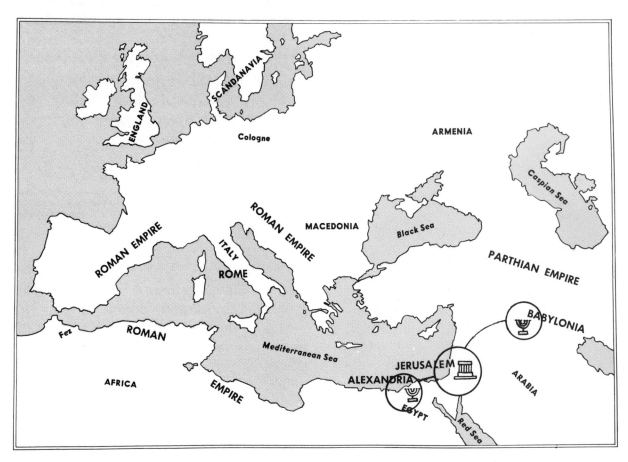

The largest Jewish communities are encircled; the city of Alexandria in Egypt, the land of Israel itself and the center of Babylon.

the *Galut,* the exile. They sent money to Jerusalem to support the Temple, and, if they could, they visited the Temple and the Holy Land of their fathers.

Those who wished to study Torah always traveled to Palestine, for it was only there that the great schools taught the Law. The most famous of the Babylonian scholars, who left his home and lived in poverty in order to study in Jerusalem, was Hillel. This gentle and beloved scholar remained in Palestine and became head of the leading school and of the Sanhedrin (30 B.C.E.) . Hillel, like all the Pharisees, studied both the Written and the Oral traditions. He showed how the Oral laws

really came from the laws of the written Torah. He always interpreted the laws more kindly than his friend Shammai, the other great sage of his time.

JESUS AND HIS FOLLOWERS

Soon after the time of Hillel lived Jesus of Nazareth, whose Hebrew name would have been Joshua ben Joseph. There are no definite Jewish records of his life. From the Christian Bible, we can see him as a traveling teacher who spoke of the coming kingdom of God and inspired a small group to follow him.

The hope for a *Messiah,* a messenger sent

by God who would save the world, was very great in those troubled times. Jesus spoke of living a pure life, trusting in God, and not fighting against evil, since God would welcome the poor and the persecuted into the kingdom of heaven. Some began to call him the Messiah.

When Jesus was crucified on Passover (29 C.E.) by order of procurator Pontius Pilate, it was because he was considered to be a rebel against Rome. The Romans claimed that he wanted to be King of the Jews. Thousands of Jewish and non-Jewish rebels who had disturbed the peace of the Roman Empire suffered the same terrible death.

It was some years later, when Paul decided to bring the message of Jesus to the pagans, that Christianity began to grow throughout the world. Paul, a Greek Jew by birth, traveled throughout the Roman Empire, preaching that men would be saved by believing in Jesus as the savior. Paul told the pagans that they could serve the one God of the Jews without following the difficult Jewish laws. Eventually the Christian religion became the religion of most of the Roman Empire.

THE GREAT DESTRUCTION

The rule of the procurators in Judea became more and more harsh. Taxation was heavy and the poor became poorer. What aroused the Jews most, however, was the dishonor shown to their Temple and their religion. When the procurator Florus robbed the Temple and a crowd gathered to protest, he set his soldiers upon the people, killing thousands.

The rebellion had begun. Leaders of the Sanhedrin made plans for war. They appointed military leaders, the most important being Josephus (38-100), who was expected to hold back the Roman legions in Galilee in the north.

Emperor Nero sent three legions under his best general, Vespasian, who became emperor himself soon after Galilee fell into Roman hands. General Josephus gave up and went over to the Roman side. Though a traitor, Josephus is important because later he wrote a great book on Jewish history, from which we learn much that is recorded nowhere else.

Jewish forces gathered in Jerusalem for the final desperate fight. The Roman legions, first under Vespasian and then under his son Titus, besieged the city. No food or water could go in. Inside the starving city, the Zealots would not allow anyone to talk of surrender or of making peace.

The Romans breached the city walls with their battering rams. They fought through the streets until they came to the area of the Temple itself, also surounded by a wall. On the 17th day of *Tammuz,* the Temple service had to stop, for there was nothing left to

Coin of the Emperor Vespasian, struck in Palestine, with the inscription "Judaea Devicta."

sacrifice and the war raged around its walls. For three heroic and hopeless weeks the defenders held out in the Temple itself.

On the ninth day of *Av,* in the year 70, the Romans stormed the walls and set the Temple on fire. This was the darkest day in Jewish history, remembered ever after as a fast day. The legionnaires killed every defender, and grabbed as prizes the *Menorahs* and beautiful adornments of the Temple.

Though fighting was now useless, groups of Zealots held out longer. The last fortress to fall was Masada on the shore of the Dead

Masada, this fortress high on a rock near the Dead Sea, was the last Jewish stronghold to fall to the Roman conquerors following the destruction of the Temple.

Sea. There the defenders killed themselves rather than surrender to the Romans.

Josephus tells of the terrible slaughter. Hundreds of thousands were killed, or sold into slavery all over the world. Titus was so

A copy of the carving on the Arch of Titus, showing the Menorah and other furniture of the Temple being carried in triumph through the streets of Rome.

proud of his difficult victory over this small country that he led a victory parade through Rome. Jewish captives in chains carried the Menorahs through the streets of the enemy. The government struck coins bearing the words *Judaea capta:* "Judea is taken." The Arch of Titus, built to celebrate the triumph, still stands today in the ruins of the Roman Forum.

THE SCHOOL AT YAVNEH

There is a story that while the Romans were besieging Jerusalem, the scholar Johanan ben Zakkai wanted to speak to the Roman commander. The Zealots would not let anyone leave the city. Therefore his students claimed that he was dead, hid him in a coffin, and carried him outside the city walls, supposedly for burial.

Once outside the city, Johanan was able to speak to Vespasian. He asked for one favor— that he be allowed to start a school in the

A building thought to be the tomb of Johanan ben Zakkai, near Tiberias on the shore of Lake Kineret in Israel.

town of Yavneh near the Mediterranean Sea. The Roman gave permission.

The school that Johanan started was what saved the Jewish people. Though their Temple was destroyed and tremendous numbers of their people were lost, the study of the Torah continued and the faith of the Jews became stronger.

Johanan and his school carried on the work of Hillel, interpreting the laws, explaining how each rule in the Oral Law was derived from the Torah. They taught the Jews how they could continue to be Jews without the Temple and its services, by keeping the laws of the Torah in their daily lives.

THE LAST REBELLION

Rome continued its plans of conquering the world. The emperor Trajan tried to take over the Parthian kingdom. The Jews of that part of the world fought against him. There were Jewish revolts also in Egypt and in Cyprus. Trajan tried to get the Jews to his side by promising to rebuild the Temple.

A silver coin issued by the revolutionary government of Bar Kochba. He and his followers set up a Jewish state (132-135) which was soon crushed by the Romans.

The promise was not kept. Hadrian, who followed Trajan as emperor, came to Jerusalem and ordered that the holy city be rebuilt as a pagan capital, with a temple dedicated to Jupiter, chief of the pagan gods.

This the Jews would not tolerate. The aged Rabbi Akiva, greatest teacher of his time, and a worker for peace all his life, was the leading spirit in the rebellion which now arose.

The military leader was Simeon Bar Kochba, a brave and loyal Jew who seemed like another Judah Maccabee to his people. He and his troops captured Jerusalem and built an altar on the Temple mount.

Hadrian sent a powerful army, led by his best general. For two years they fought against Bar Kochba's troops, blocking supplies from reaching Jerusalem, and finally driving the rebels into the town of Betar. When Betar fell (135), betrayed by spies, thousands of Jewish fighters, including Bar Kochba, were killed.

THE PERSECUTIONS OF HADRIAN

More than half a million Jews lost their lives in this last heroic rebellion. In that terrible time, Hadrian decided to put an end to this stubborn people. He had decreed that no Jew could circumcise his son, keep the Sabbath or holidays, or study or teach the Torah. All these deeds were now to be punishable by death.

Rabbi Akiva was one of the many who became martyrs, giving their lives to keep and to teach the Law. Because of leaders like him, and the devotion of the masses of the people, Judaism did not die out.

After some years of persecution, while the Jews kept their faith as well as they could in secret, the Romans stopped carrying out the laws of Hadrian. The Jewish people no longer had the numbers nor the spirit to revolt. Indeed, they had come to realize that it was going to be their tradition and their way of life that would keep them alive as a people, and not their own national state.

SYNAGOGUES AND ACADEMIES

After the loss of the Temple, the synagogues which had been built in each town and community became the chief meeting places and centers of worship for the Jews. Regular prayers were said morning and afternoon, in which the Temple worship was recalled. The study of the Torah became the central part of the service on Sabbath and holy days. Thus, prayer and study rather than sacrifice became the way the Jew showed his devotion to God.

Study was the basis of Jewish life. The rabbis of the academies decided on questions of Jewish law. Johanan ben Zakkai had reinstated the *Bet Din,* or religious court. The head of the court was called the *Nasi,* meaning prince or president; and descendants of Hillel were appointed to this honored position, which was even recognized by Rome.

Remains of the well-preserved synagogue at Kfar Nahum, or Capernaum, in Israel. It was built in the second century, and may have been known to Judah Ha-Nasi.

The Nasi was also called Patriarch.

Though everything was interrupted during the disastrous rebellion and the persecution of Hadrian, the academies were allowed to reopen in the year 150. The leaders in the academies, all rabbis and sages, were called *Tannaim,* from a word meaning "to teach." They knew that war, persecution and exile might cause the Jewish people to forget their law, unless it was carefully gathered together and written down in one place. The old feeling about keeping the Oral Law unwritten was no longer followed.

The greatest Patriarch was Judah Ha-Nasi, who had enough wisdom and authority to edit all the independent *Mishnayot,* statements of the Oral Law, and organize them into six Orders of the *Mishnah* (200).

The Mishnah became the book of study for all Jewish schools. Scholars called *Amoraim,* a word coming from the root "to speak," discussed the Mishnah and added commentary to it. The discussions were later gathered into the *Gemara.* The Mishnah together with its long commentary, the Gemara, became the *Talmud.* There are two Talmuds; one is the Jerusalem Talmud, or *Talmud Yerushalmi.*

The community in Palestine, however, had become weaker; and the community in Babylonia, stronger. Rav and Samuel were two Babylonian Jews who came to study with Judah Ha-Nasi and returned to found schools in their home country. They took with them the Mishnah. For two hundred years and more, the Amoraim of Babylonia discussed the Mishnah and all the traditions of Jewish life and history. The Gemara thus created was put together first by Rav Ashi, and then in final form by Rabina, producing the tremendous many-volume work, the *Talmud Bavli,* Babylonian Talmud.

By the year 500, when the Talmud had been compiled, the last Nasi of the house of

A page of the Talmud with some of the commentaries. The selection is from Baba Kamma, first tractate of the Order Nezikim. The Talmudic passage is in the center island, the lines of Mishnah being followed by the Gemara beginning on the fourteenth line. To the left is the commentary of Rashi, and to the right, that of the Tosafists.

Hillel had died. The Roman government was supposed to appoint a Patriarch. But meanwhile, the rulers of Rome, beginning with the emperor Constantine in 325, had become Christian. The bishops of the Christian church persuaded the emperor not to appoint a new Patriarch at all. The Jews should not have any rights or any power in the Holy Land, said the bishops, for they had refused to accept Christianity. The growing church wanted to convert the world.

Babylonia, not being under Christian rule, and not being affected by the many wars that attended the breakup of the Roman Empire, was a safer and more peaceful place than Palestine. The Jews there were a comparatively favored community for centuries, and were able to give leadership to other Jews all over the world.

The Jews were not united in one country or under one government. The most important community might be now in one land, now in another. Persecutions weakened one group while another prospered for a while. Whole communities might be destroyed or exiled in any of the many lands where the Jews found themselves.

The Jewish people, however, lived on, bound together by one way of life, which was prescribed for them in the Talmud, united also in remembrance of the past and hope for the "end of days" when God would bless His people and all mankind with peace.

The Arch of Constantine in the Roman Forum. Such monuments were erected to glorify emperors and generals who had won great victories. The Arch of Titus is nearby.

THE TALMUDIC AGE

SOFERIM (*scribes*)
**Fifth to Third
centuries B.C.E.**

The generations of scholars and teachers who carried on the work of EZRA.

ZUGOT (*pairs*)
**Second century
B.C.E. until
about 10 C.E.**

The two leaders of the great Sanhedrin who carried on the teachings and interpretations of the Torah after the period of the Soferim. HILLEL and SHAMMAI were the last and most brilliant of the Zugot.

TANNAIM (*teachers*)
**First and Second
centuries C.E.**

The scholars and teachers whose works are recorded in the Mishnah.

41 GAMALIEL I, Nasi and last president of the Great Sanhedrin.

70 JOHANAN BEN ZAKKAI, founder of the academy of Javneh.

80 GAMALIEL II, Nasi and head of the Sanhedrin and of the academy at Javneh.

130 RABBI AKIVA.

138 RABBI MEIR and SIMEON BAR YOHAI.

165–200 JUDAH HA-NASI (Judah I), Nasi, head of the Sanhedrin and the academy, compiler of the Mishnah.

AMORAIM (*speakers*)
**Third to Sixth
centuries C.E.
(about 200-499)**

The scholars and teachers whose work is recorded in the Gemara.

210 GAMALIEL III, son of Judah Ha-Nasi, head of the academy and of the Sanhedrin.

219 *ABBA AREKHA (RAV) and MAR SAMUEL founded the Babylonian Talmud.

225 JOHANAN BAR NAPPAHA and SIMEON BEN LAKHISH.

259 HILLEL II, Nasi and head of the academy and of the Sanhedrin, introduced the fixed calendar.

370 Completion of the Palestinian Talmud.

425 GAMALIEL IV, last Nasi. End of Patriarchate.

354–427 *ASHI and

499 RABINA, compiled the Babylonian Talmud.

SABORAIM (*reasoners*)
500 until 530 C.E.

The scholars and teachers who completed the editing of the Babylonian Talmud. Until the time of the Gaonate great Babylonian scholars bore the title of SABORA.

This chart refers to only a few of the many Talmudic scholars. Babylonian scholars are marked with an asterisk*.

Hillel

First Century B.C.E.

In the city of Jerusalem, two thousand years ago, a pagan stood before a Jew.

A pagan is one who does not know the one true God of the universe, but worships many gods. He may pray to idols, to trees or rivers, to animals, to sun or moon or stars. He may think that there are hundreds of gods in human form; and that each country or even each family has its own special god to take care of it.

Where this particular pagan came from, we do not know. He may have been a Roman, brought up to worship Jupiter or Mars; for the Roman Empire ruled over Jerusalem, and many of its soldiers were stationed there. He may have been a Greek, praying to Zeus, king of the gods; for Greeks lived in many cities of the world, and in Alexandria, for instance, he might have met many Jews and heard of their faith.

He might have come from any country of the world, for the entire world was pagan at that time. Out of the land of Israel, the little country the Romans called Judea, came the knowledge of one God.

At any rate, the pagan had come to Jerusalem. Like many of his friends, he had wondered about the truth of all the gods he had heard of at home. He saw that the worship

of many gods brought people not to n deeds but to selfishness and hatred of oth not to peace but to war. Some of his frie may have converted to Judaism, become lowers of the Jewish religion. He had c to Jerusalem to seek out the leading tea of the Jews and learn what this faith wa about.

He had heard that it took a long tim learn enough to be a Jew. He was, howe an impatient man. He wanted his an quickly. He came first to the house of Sl mai, one of the two great teachers of the J

"I am interested in becoming a Jew, said. Shammai, who was busy measu something with a ruler, looked at him waited. "I am willing to be a Jew," saic stranger, "if you can teach me the w Torah while I stand on one foot."

Shammai raised his hand, with the me ing stick in it, and shook it angrily a questioner. "Are you trying to make fu me and of the Torah?" he asked. "Get o my sight!" The pagan ducked to escap stick and ran away.

He had heard there was another tea as great as Shammai. He soon found the l of Hillel. "What do you wish, my son?" : Hillel.

"I would like to become a Jew, if yo teach me the Torah while I stand on foot," said the pagan.

Hillel smiled. "I will give you the L; one sentence," he said. "Whatever is ha to you, do not do to your neighbor. Th of the laws are all commentary on this Go now and study."

The pagan was so impressed by this ar that he went and studied seriously, an came a loyal Jew.

This was the way of the gentle Hillel, beloved of teachers.

Old city wall in Jerusalem.

The Young Student

Hillel himself had not learned the Torah quickly or easily. He studied all his life. In Babylonia, where he was born, he had learned all he could. Then, though he had little money and the journey was long, he had come to Palestine to hear the wisdom of the famous teachers Shemaiah and Avtalion. He worked as a woodchopper to support himself while a student.

There is a favorite story about the young Hillel. It tells how he worked hard at his task as a woodchopper, and received very little pay. Half of his income used to go to the doorkeeper at the school, who would not let anyone in without payment.

One day Hillel found himself without a single coin. He knew the doorkeeper would not let him in, but he could not bear the thought of missing one day of school. In the roof of the building was a window, and to this he climbed. Lying across the skylight, he could hear faintly the words of the scholars below.

It was a winter day, unusually cold for Jerusalem. Snow began to fall. Hillel, fascina-

A sofer, or scribe, writing in the traditional way in which scrolls of the Torah and other holy works have been set down since the days of the Second Temple.

ted by the lesson, did not move from his place. It was Friday, and the Sabbath came.

In the morning, the two teachers noticed that it was darker than it should be in the study room. Looking up, they saw a form blocking the skylight. They rushed to the roof and found the young man lying there frozen and still.

They carried him down, warmed oil over the fire and rubbed it on his frozen limbs. "For some one as devoted to study as this, it would even be permitted to break the Sabbath," they said.

From that time on, Hillel was welcomed without paying any fee, and the greedy doorkeeper was made to change his ways.

The Written Law and the Oral Law

What was it that Hillel had come to study? He had read all the books of the Bible, but, like all the Jews, he especially studied the first five, the books of Moses, telling of the creation of the world and the beginnings of the Jewish people. These five books were already being read the year round in the synagogues of Palestine and Babylonia, as they are to this day. They are called the Torah, meaning "Teaching" or "Law," for they contain all the commandments of God which Moses taught to the children of Israel on their way from Egypt to the Promised Land.

There was more to Jewish life, however, than keeping the written laws of the Torah. From the beginning there had grown up among the Jewish people laws and customs that helped them obey the commandments of the Torah.

The Torah commands that the Jews rest on the Sabbath day, and find delight in it. It does not spell out exactly how one ought to rest, or what is the proper way to spend the Sabbath. The people, with the aid of their teachers, came to understand the different kinds of

A young Israeli student reading on a stone bench at Capernaum where the sages of the Talmud may have sat.

activity that should not be allowed on the Sabbath, and the way one should make the Sabbath a delight by fine clothes and good meals, by saying *Kiddush* and lighting candles, by prayers and study together with fellow Jews.

The Torah contains many commandments about love for fellow man, kindness and charity, and justice for poor and rich alike. But there are no instructions for the actual way to set up a court and to conduct a trial. Such matters had to be worked out by the people and their leaders.

The many, many laws and customs which had grown up out of the commandments of the Torah were called the Unwritten Torah. It can also be called the Oral Torah or Oral Law, for "oral" means "spoken," and this tradition was taught by teacher to pupil, by father to son, for many generations, always by word of mouth.

Although this tradition was not written down, great teachers had kept the people from forgetting it. The prophets reminded the people of what God wanted them to do. The First Temple had been destroyed, and the Jews sent into exile; but when they re-

turned to build the Second Temple, the teacher Ezra had instructed them once more in their history and the rules of their faith. Scholars in each generation continued to explain the law. Eventually the Sanhedrin, the great court of seventy-one scholars, taught and judged the people.

Even war was once needed to allow the Jews to remain faithful to their laws. This was when the Maccabees fought against the armies of King Antiochus. The king wanted to make the Jews pagans, like the Greeks, and ordered the Temple to be used for the worship of idols. He commanded the Jews to eat forbidden food, to pray to Greek gods and to forget their own holy days. Judah Maccabee and his brothers fought for the right of the Jews to keep their laws, and won the victory we celebrate on Hanukkah.

Hillel the Elder

In the time of Hillel, the Maccabees were remembered. Members of their family, the Hasmoneans, had been ruling the Jews of Palestine. They had been successful in war and had added the country of Edom to the land of Israel.

During Hillel's life, the reign of the Hasmoneans came to an end. Herod, who was appointed king of Judea by the Roman rulers, was, in fact, the descendant of Edomites. He was a strong and cruel king, who killed even members of his own family to gain more power. He built cities and rebuilt the

A coin of King Herod with the name of the city of Tiberias and the legend "Herod the Tetrarch."

Temple, making it bigger and more glorious. But he was not respected or loved by the Jewish people.

Hillel, who became head of his school and was appointed by Herod to rule the Sanhedrin, was the true leader of the people. He was called Hillel the Elder. He did, indeed, live a long life and continued to teach for forty years. The name "Elder," however, was given because of the respect the people had for him, for he was like a father to them all.

"A bad tempered man cannot be a good teacher," said Hillel. A story told about him shows his kindness and patience.

A man made a bet with a friend, to the amount of four hundred silver coins, that he could make Hillel angry.

Late Friday afternoon, as Hillel was washing himself for the Sabbath, the man banged on Hillel's door and shouted, "Hillel, are you in there?"

Hillel put on a robe and came to the door. "What do you wish, my son?" he asked.

"I have a question for you," said the man.

"Ask your question, my son," said Hillel.

"Why do the Babylonians have queer-shaped heads?" asked the man.

Hillel, who was a Babylonian himself, did not mind the insult. "That is a difficult question, my son," he answered. "It must be because the women who attend the babies when they are born are not skilled."

The man left without a word. Soon he came back again, shouting, "Hillel, where are you?" Hillel came out again and said, "What do you wish, my son?"

"I have another question," said the man. "Ask it, my son," said Hillel.

"Why do the people of Tadmor have weak eyes?" the man asked.

"That is a very good question," answered the sage. "It is because they live where sand is always blowing into their eyes."

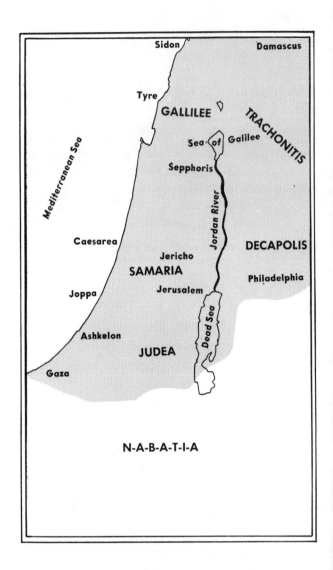

Map of Israel during the time of Hillel.

The man went away and again returned. "Hillel, come out!" he called. Hillel came out and asked, "What do you wish, my son?"

"I have a question for you," the man said.

"Ask it and I will try to answer," said Hillel.

"Why do the Africans have broad feet?" asked the man.

26

"That is a fine question. The Africans have broad feet so that they may walk well on swampy ground. Now, do you have any more questions?"

The man tried once more to win his bet. "Are you the Hillel who is called prince of Israel?"

"I am," said Hillel.

"I wish there might be no more like you in Israel," said the man in disgust.

"Why?" asked Hillel gently.

"Because by keeping your temper you have made me lose a bet of four hundred *zuzim*," the man complained.

"Better that you should lose four hundred zuzim," said Hillel, "than that I should lose my temper."

Hillel and Shammai

Shammai was a friend of Hillel, a scholar equally as brilliant, and the leader of another school. Both were Pharisees, the name given to those scholars who taught the Oral Law to the people. Most of the members of the Sanhedrin belonged to this group, which said that all Jews, young and old, poor or rich, must study and keep both the Written and the Oral Law. The Pharisees insisted that every town must have a school, and every child must learn.

The Sadducees, another group of that time, did not value education for all, or the development of the law among the people. They were mostly of wealthy or priestly families, and stressed the Temple service and the authority of the ruling class more than the daily life of the Jew.

Though Hillel and Shammai agreed about the importance of the whole of Jewish law, teaching it and living by it with all their might, they were different one from the other. Shammai was stern and strict. If there were two ways of following a law, Shammai would

Entrance to a tomb thought to be that of Hillel the Elder.

insist on the harder way. Hillel was more easygoing.

The kindly nature of Hillel is shown in a difference of opinion between the two scholars. At weddings, it was the custom to sing songs and say poems before the bride, telling how lovely she was. Shammai was asked if this was permitted if the bride was not really beautiful. Would it not be telling a lie?

Shammai answered sternly, "You may speak only the exact truth. Describe the bride as she is."

Hillel answered, "You may always say the bride is lovely and good."

Although they and their students after them disagreed on many points, Hillel and Shammai agreed on the most important things. They wished the life of the Jews to be fine and good. They knew that study of the law and following the law through every day of their lives would make them a holy people.

Shammai said, "Assign for yourself a definite time for study every day." Hillel agreed: "Do not say, when I have free time I will study. You may never have leisure."

In almost every case of two opinions, the decision of Hillel was the one the people fol-

Title page from the Soncino Hebrew-English Talmud, new edition of the great work which Hillel began.

lowed. The teachings of Shammai, however, were considered equally true. "Both the words of Hillel and the words of Shammai are inspired by God," said the scholars.

Interpreting the Law

Hillel's teaching showed how the Oral Law came from the Written Law. He listed ways in which a rule might be based on a sentence in the Torah. Explaining the words of the Torah and showing what lessons can be learned from them is called interpretation. Hillel was one of the great interpreters of the Torah.

The Jews sometimes found it difficult to follow the commandments. A merchant came to Hillel, saying, "I must borrow money every few years to send out ships and buy things to sell. I am able to pay back the money after I sell my stock at a profit. But, as you know, the Torah commands that in the seventh year, the Sabbath year, all debts be cancelled.

"If I try to borrow money at a time near the year of release, no one will lend it to me, because they know they cannot get it back. In the time of the giving of the Torah, most people were farmers. They did not carry on business in this way. Now my business depends on loans."

Hillel studied the law and all the traditions concerning it. He knew that the court can decide where unclaimed money is to go. He tried to interpret the law for the benefit of all the people.

Hillel interpreted the law, showing that the lender could make a special statement to the court, saying that the judges of the court were to collect the debt. Then he could take his money back even after the seventh year. This helped both those who needed to borrow money, and those who lent money and might have failed to collect it. Now the people could follow the law of the Torah which says that it is forbidden to refuse to lend money near the time of release.

Hillel was admired for his kindness and patience, for his friendliness and gentle nature. He was never proud, though he was the most honored scholar of his time. His influence lived long after him.

Johanan ben Zakkai, the best pupil in the school of Hillel, became the leading scholar of the next generation. Through establishing a school at Yavneh, and appointing a Bet Din, a court of Jewish law, Johanan taught the Jews how to live according to their laws after the Temple was destroyed by Rome.

The name of Hillel was so respected that it seemed right that Hillel's great-grandson, Gamaliel, and his descendants after him, should be chosen to head the Sanhedrin.

Above all his other virtues, Hillel's love for learning has been an example to Jewish students to this day. His words to the pagan have always been remembered.

The kindly scholar knew that love of neighbor and justice to fellow man were the purpose of all Jewish law. But his own lifetime of study showed that to be a good Jew, it is not enough to know the general idea of the religion. It is necessary to know how to live by the rule every day of one's life.

His message to the pagan is a message for us to this day:

"The rest of the laws are all commentary on the law to love your fellowman. Now go and study!"

SAYINGS OF HILLEL

Do not separate yourself from the community.

*   *   *

Do not judge your fellowman until you have been in his place.

*   *   *

A fool cannot keep from sinning, and an ignorant man cannot be a saint; a shy person cannot learn, and an impatient man cannot teach; he who spends all his time on business will not become wise. In a place where there are no men, try to be a man.

*   *   *

If I am not for myself, who will be for me? And if I am for myself only, what am I? And if not now, when?

*   *   *

Reviewing a lesson a hundred times is not as good as reviewing it a hundred and one times.

*   *   *

God the Merciful turns the scale of judgment toward mercy.

*   *   *

God says, "If you come to My house, I will come to yours."

*   *   *

When his students asked him if it is a religious deed to take a bath: Yes, for the man who is appointed to wash and polish the statues of the king which are set up in public places receives a salary and high honor for doing so; how much more must I take good care of my body, since it is created in the image of God.

*   *   *

The more wealth, the more worry; the more servants, the more idleness; the more possessions, the more loss; the more study of the Law, the more life; the more learning, the more wisdom; the more righteousness, the more peace.

*   *   *

Leave it to the people. If they are not prophets, they are the sons of prophets.

*   *   *

Be a follower of Aaron, loving peace and pursuing peace, loving thy fellowmen, and drawing them near to the Torah.

Akiva

40 - 135

An ignorant man and then a scholar, a lover of peace who became leader of a revolution, an honored sage who became a heroic martyr —this was Akiva, rabbi and teacher in Israel.

Many stories have been told of Akiva's long and exciting life. The tale of how he became the leading scholar of his time is one of the finest romances ever written.

It is said that Akiva, till the age of forty, was a shepherd who did not even know how to read and write. Rachel, the daughter of the wealthy man whose flock he tended, met him and fell in love with him. She wanted to marry him in spite of his ignorance and low station, because she was sure he could become a great man.

The father was furious, and made a vow that if his daughter married such an ignoramus, he would never speak to her or give her any help. Nevertheless, the two were married. They lived in poverty.

Rachel encouraged her husband to study, but he felt it was a hopeless task. One day he noticed a stone at the edge of a well, which had been hollowed out by drippings from the water bucket. "If these drops of water, year after year, can wear away solid stone," thought Akiva, "then surely patient studying of the word of God can make an impression on my mind." He resolved to go to study at the academy of Eliezer and Joshua, who were carrying on the work of their teacher, Johanan ben Zakkai.

Not only did Rachel consent to his going away, but, the story goes, she even cut off and sold her hair to a wig-merchant in order to pay for his going. Though she had children by this time, and had to support them herself, she was willing to make any sacrifice in order for her husband to become a learned man.

Akiva stayed away twelve years. By the end of that time, he had indeed become the best student at the school, and was able to explain

Bas relief of the Ark of the Law, sculptured in rock at the Synagogue of Capernaum.

points of the law better than his teachers. He returned home.

Outside the poor hovel he paused. He heard voices from within. A neighbor was scolding his wife Rachel.

"See how you have to live! It's time you went to the academy and demanded that your husband come home after all these years."

Rachel answered gently, "If I had my way, he would stay at the academy another twelve years."

Akiva, so the story tells us, turned away and returned to his studies.

At the end of another twelve years, Akiva returned to his home once more. This time he came as a great teacher and scholar, followed by thousands of students. The people of the town crowded around to see the famous man.

A poorly-dressed woman tried to come near to Rabbi Akiva. His students wanted to push her away. The rabbi descended from his place and took the woman's hand, for it was Rachel. "Give her honor," he said, "for all that I know, and all that you have learned from me, are owed to this noble woman."

Those who had problems to solve came to

see the visiting scholar. Among them was an old man, dressed in fine clothing but sorrowful in appearance.

"Many years ago," he said to the rabbi, "I made a vow. I am old and have not many years left. I am sorry for the vow, and I would like to know if I could possibly be released from it."

"What was this vow you made?" asked Rabbi Akiva.

"When my daughter enraged me by marrying a poor shepherd," said the man, "I swore never to speak to her or to give her any help."

"For what reason did you make this vow?" asked Rabbi Akiva.

"Because he was an ignorant man who could not even read or write," said the elderly man.

"Vows cannot be easily broken," said the rabbi, "but this was a vow made because of a certain condition. If the condition has changed, the vow need no longer be kept. You may consider your vow null and void, because I am that same ignorant shepherd."

Rachel's father rejoiced to recognize his distinguished son-in-law, and to embrace his long-lost daughter and his grandchildren.

Wealthy and respected, leader and teacher of his people, Akiva never forgot to give credit to Rachel. Answering the question, "Who is really a rich man?" Akiva said, "He who has a good wife."

Rabbi and Teacher

Akiva is included as one of the Tannaim, teachers of the Oral Law, as were Hillel and Shammai, Johanan ben Zakkai, Akiva's teachers Eliezer and Joshua, and other great scholars of their time. Because of the fact that the Jews no longer had their own government, and Roman and other foreign influences were all around, Akiva felt that the Law was

An old stone building near Lake Kineret or Tiberias which is supposed to house the tomb of the great sage Rabbi Meir.

more important than ever to keep the Jews together.

"Arrange the laws in order, like a set table," said Rabbi Akiva. He was the first to organize the traditions of the Jews. First he helped decide with other scholars the order of the books of the Bible. With them he decided that later works, written in the time of the Maccabees and even after, should not be considered holy like the earlier writings.

Then Akiva and his school, particularly his best student, Rabbi Meir, started to put into order all the laws and opinions, and all the interpretations of the Torah that had come down through the years in the oral tradition.

Akiva was a remarkable interpreter of the Torah. There is a strange legend that tells that Moses, receiving the Torah from the hand of God, noticed that the letters had tiny crowns and decorations on them. Moses asked God the meaning of these little crowns.

"There will come a scholar who will find meanings, who will build mountains of law on each of the points of these crowns," was the answer.

The legend continues that Moses asked if he could look into the future and see this great scholar. His wish was granted, and he was able in spirit to look in on a class conducted by Rabbi Akiva. As the great teacher explained one law after another, Moses found he could not understand what he was talking about.

A student also was puzzled, and asked, "From where do you get the law you are describing?" Rabbi Akiva answered in surprise, "Why, this is the law of Moses that he received on Mount Sinai."

The legend illustrates how much Rabbi Akiva could learn from the smallest point in the Torah. Moses the lawgiver himself could not have foreseen it.

"Love Thy Neighbor"

Rabbi Akiva was a man of mercy as well as of justice. He was well known as a giver of charity, even saying that when a rich man had become poor, it was necessary to give him more, because he was used to luxury. He himself fulfilled, and urged his students to fulfill, such good deeds as visiting the sick.

A Roman once argued with Rabbi Akiva. "If your God wanted the poor to have food, He would give it to them. Suppose a human king was angry with his servant, and put him in prison, ordering that he was not to get food or drink. If someone went and fed the servant, and gave him drink, the king would be angry. Doesn't your God say, 'Unto me the children of Israel are servants'? Therefore He would not want you to give charity to the poor, whom He has made to suffer."

Rabbi Akiva answered, "I will give you a different example. Suppose a human king was angry with his son, imprisoned him and ordered that he get no food or drink. Then someone goes and gives the son food and drink. The king loves his son; will he not reward the one who helped him? We are not only servants of God; we are called His chil-

dren."

When Akiva was asked what he considered the most important law in the Torah, he answered, "Love thy neighbor as thyself."

Rebellion Against Rome

Akiva traveled to many communities, even to the city of Rome, and to Babylonia. He was well aware of the hardships his people suffered in their own homeland of Palestine. The Romans had destroyed their Temple. Still in the memory of the people was the terrible destruction that resulted from the rebellion against Rome sixty years before.

When rash leaders tried to urge another uprising against the Roman rulers, Akiva always advised peace. Despite harsh laws and heavy taxes, the Jews were allowed to live according to the laws of their religion. Akiva felt that a revolution would only bring on worse destruction.

There came a time when the Jews were filled with hope. They heard that the new emperor, Hadrian, was going to have the Temple in Jerusalem rebuilt. Rejoicing turned to shock when Hadrian announced that Jerusalem would indeed be rebuilt, but as a pagan city, with a temple devoted to the

A Latin inscription in the North African city of Cyrene, telling how the Jews had risen in rebellion against the Roman empire in the year 115. Many revolts by courageous Jews of different lands were crushed by the mighty Romans.

worship of Jupiter.

Rabbi Akiva had believed in Roman promises. Now his peace-loving nature was changed to that of a fighter. He helped to rouse the Jews to the need for a revolution against Rome.

Simeon bar Koziba, a patriotic and pious Jew, and a powerful leader, became the leader of the Judean forces. Akiva gave him every aid and support. The aged scholar saw in this young man the messenger sent by God to save the Jewish people. It was Akiva who, quoting the sentence, "A star has come forth from Jacob," gave the young hero the name of Bar Kochba, "Son of a Star."

Hundreds of thousands volunteered to fight. They were untrained as soldiers, and their weapons were as nothing compared to the Roman machines of war. Yet their faith

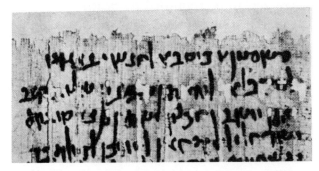
Some lines of a letter in Bar Kochba's own handwriting.

the might of the Roman Empire made itself felt.

The Roman armies attacked from all sides. With skill gained in fighting untrained revolutionaries in other parts of the Empire, they devastated the land, cut off supplies, and wore out the defenders.

Forced to give up Jerusalem, Bar Kochba and his army put up a last stand at Betar. Spies showed the Romans a secret way into town, and thousands of Jewish fighters, including their leader, were killed.

More than half a million Jews were killed in battle. There is no way of counting those who died in the towns and cities, or who were captured and sold as slaves. The rebellion had brought only disaster.

The Persecutions of Hadrian

Hadrian now felt that he could really put an end to this stubborn people. He had learned that it was their religion that made the Jews haters of Rome. It was the religion that he now attacked.

Jerusalem was built as a pagan city. Hadrian ordered that no Jews could come near it. He forbade the Jews to circumcise their sons or to teach them Torah. The Academy and the Bet Din were no longer to meet. Sabbath and holidays were not to be observed. Teaching or studying of Jewish tradition, or appointing rabbis to carry on that tradition,

A cave in which writings and coins of the Bar Kochba period have recently been found by Hebrew University archeologists. They believe it to be one of the headquarters of the revolt.

was so great that they thought they could win.

Indeed, the Jews were able to capture Jerusalem, and to hold it for two years. With brave hope, Bar Kochba proclaimed that the Third Jewish Commonwealth had been established, and that Judea was free once more. Then were acts to be punished by death.

To the credit of the leaders of that generation, they did not surrender to the severe decrees of Rome. Teaching and observing of the law continued. There are stories of young students going off to the woods with bows and arrows, taking food with them, as though they were going hunting. Once away from the town, they would study Torah.

Those really in danger were the leading teachers and scholars, for the Roman rulers kept them under watch. It is said that a friend of Rabbi Akiva found him speaking about the Torah before a large audience, and asked him, "Akiva, are you not afraid of punishment by the government?"

Akiva replied, "I will tell you a story. A fox was walking along the bank of a stream and saw some fish swimming from one place to another. He asked them, 'What are you trying to escape?' They answered, 'We are trying to escape the nets of the fishermen.' The fox said, 'Then why don't you come up on dry land, where I am, and live with me? For there is no danger of nets up here.'

"The fish replied, 'Are you supposed to be the cleverest of animals? You are a fool. If we are in danger in the water, which is the only place we can live, how much more so in a place where we cannot live at all!'

Roman sculpture of Emperor Hadrian.

"So it is with us," said Akiva. "While we study Torah, which is our life and the length of our days, we may be in danger; but how much more so if we forsake the source of our life!"

Akiva the Martyr

Akiva was arrested and put in prison. The Romans wanted to make an example of this leader and sage, and condemned him to death.

The aged scholar was brought out and tortured by having his flesh torn by iron combs. Through it all he did not cry out. The Roman jailer could not understand it. "Is this magic," he asked, "that you don't feel any pain?"

"I feel pain," said Akiva, "but I am happy. All my life I have been reading 'Thou shalt love the Lord thy God with all thy heart, and with all thy soul, and with all thy might.' Now at last I am really fulfilling that commandment."

The last words of Akiva were the words of the *Shema:* "Hear O Israel, the Lord thy God, the Lord is One."

The time came when the persecutions of Hadrian ended. The Jews were once more permitted to practice their faith, and to open the doors of their academies. It was the teaching and the martyrdom of Akiva and others who followed him that kept the faith of the people alive until that day.

Not all the efforts of Akiva and Bar Kochba could restore the Jews to their kingdom at that time. But in the kingdom of mind and spirit, and in a way of life that continued despite all disaster, the efforts of Rabbi Akiva were crowned with victory.

SAYINGS OF RABBI AKIVA

"Thou shalt love thy neighbor as thyself." You should not, however, say that since I am hated, let my fellowman be hated with me; since I am cursed, let my fellowman also be cursed. For if you show hatred to any man, you are in truth despising the Creator, who made man.

* * *

Take your seat a little below your rank, for it is better to be asked to come up than to be told to go down.

* * *

What is the best offering to God? Charity to His children.

* * *

Beloved is man, for he was created in the image of God; still greater was the love, in that it was made known to him that he was so created. Beloved is Israel, for they are called the children of God. Beloved is Israel, presented with the most precious treasure (the Torah), by which the world was created.

* * *

All Jews are of royal descent. Even the poor among them are noblemen, for they are children of Abraham, Isaac and Jacob.

* * *

Study is greater than practice, because study leads to practice.

* * *

As a house implies a builder, a dress a weaver, a door a carpenter, so the world proclaims God, its Creator.

* * *

Whatever the All-merciful does is for good. In pleasure or pain, give thanks.

* * *

When Rabbi Akiva was on a journey, he came to a town and asked for a place to sleep, but was refused. He said, "Whatever the All-merciful does is for the best," and went to sleep in the woods.

    He had with him a rooster, a donkey on which to ride, and a lamp to light his way. The wind blew out the lamp; a cat came and ate the rooster, and a lion killed the donkey. He said, "Whatever the All-merciful does is for the best." That same night a band of robbers came and killed everyone who was sleeping in the town. Because he had no light, and no donkey or rooster to make noise, they did not find him.

Judah Ha-Nasi

135 - 220

In the same year, and perhaps on the very day that Rabbi Akiva met his death, a son was born to Rabbi Simon ben Gamaliel, descendant of Hillel. The mother and father should have been overjoyed at the birth of their first child. Instead, they hid the news of his birth as well as they could, and spoke in fear.

"At this terrible time," said the father, "who can tell what will be the fate of our child? Even to circumcise him now is against the laws of the Romans. I have always looked forward to teaching my children Torah, as my father taught me. Now the teaching of Torah is a crime against Rome, punishable by death."

Remains of the entrance to the tomb of Judah Ha-Nasi.

"We must have faith," said the mother. "There have been dark days before in the history of our people. This persecution cannot last forever."

"No, it cannot," said the father. "The government of Rome keeps changing; one ruler is killed and another takes over; thus has it been since the time of the first Caesar. A new ruler may change the harsh decrees of the old."

"And our son may grow up even to see the Temple restored," said the mother, "and the Jews ruling themselves in their own land."

With this pious hope, the parents of young Judah, at risk of their lives, began to raise their son in accordance with Jewish law.

Their faith was rewarded. Soon the oppressive laws were changed. Academies of learning were open once more. The Romans allowed the Sanhedrin to meet again as a court of religious law. The head of the court was once again to be called the Patriarch, the leader of the Jews of Palestine; by the Jews themselves he was called, in Hebrew, *Nasi,* meaning prince.

Rabbi Simon, like his father and grandfather before him, became the Patriarch, or Nasi. He presided over the school at Usha.

Judah the Student

Young Judah studied not only in his father's school, but also in the schools of other great scholars, students of Rabbi Akiva. They had survived the terrible period of war and oppression. One of them, Simon ben Yohai, had hidden in a cave for years to escape death at the hands of the Romans. Now that the persecution was over, he was free to teach once more.

From these scholars, Judah learned Jewish tradition both Written and Oral. He studied the interpretations of the law as put forth by the Tannaim, great teachers from the time of his ancestor, Hillel, until his day.

From his teachers, also, Judah heard tales of suffering and martyrdom, of cruel laws which forbade the study of Jewish tradition, of disasters which might have put an end to the Jewish people.

"It is no longer safe," said Judah, "to depend on the memory of our teachers. A tyrant

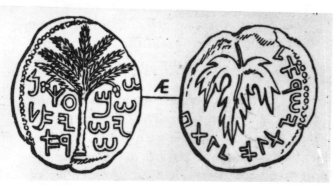

A bronze coin struck by the government of Bar Kochba, inscribed "First Year of the Redemption of Israel" and "Simon Nasi Israel." The revolution lasted from 132 to 135 and was then crushed by Rome.

could destroy all our teachers or exile all our people. The Oral Law must be collected."

As the son of the leading family of the country, Judah was raised almost like a prince. Instead of Aramaic, his family always spoke the pure Hebrew of the Bible in their home. Because Judah was expected to be a spokesman for his people, he was trained also in the speaking of Greek and Latin. His life was one of wealth and dignity.

A Menorah carved out on the wall of a tomb in Bet Shearim, in northern Israel, dating from the time of Judah Ha-Nasi. Archeologists began digging here in 1936 and have uncovered a synagogue and hundreds of tombs in the area.

Judah the Patriarch

After the death of his father, Judah became the Patriarch. More learned than his father, and trained all his life for a position of leadership, Judah Ha-Nasi became the most powerful and revered of the Patriarchs.

Students gathered in great numbers to the school of Judah Ha-Nasi at Bet Shearim. They looked up to Judah as the authority on all matters. With his wealth, he was able to maintain the school and to support students who needed help.

The hope that the kingdom of Israel would be restored did not come true in his day, but the school over which Judah presided with such honor was almost like a royal court. Judah's rule was firm. He appointed all judges and members of the Sanhedrin. Although a Roman governor ruled Palestine, Judah took on many of the tasks of governing. He opened his own storehouses to feed his followers in time of famine.

Friendship With an Emperor

Judah Ha-Nasi was the friend of a Roman emperor, probably Marcus Aurelius, who was known as a kind and intelligent ruler. There are many stories of discussions the two had, for the emperor, though a pagan, was interested in Judaism.

The emperor once challenged Rabbi Judah, saying, "How do you know you are supposed to pray three times a day? How do you know that is what God wants?"

When Judah explained to him that this was the tradition among the Jews, the emperor said, "How do you know that it would not be more pleasing to God if you prayed every hour?"

Judah said nothing, but the next day he came before the emperor, and greeted him, "Hail, great king!" An hour later he greeted him again, "All honor, mighty emperor!" When he came back an hour later, the emperor complained, "Why are you making fun of me?"

"If you, a human ruler, do not want to be praised and greeted too often, why should God desire it?" asked Rabbi Judah.

A more serious discussion is recorded, when the emperor asked, "How can there be any punishment for sins? The body can say, 'The soul is responsible for all sins, for without it I am like a stone and can do nothing.' The soul can say, 'The body commits all sins, for without it I am only a spirit which can do nothing.' "

The rabbi replied, "I will tell you a story. There was a king who had a beautiful garden, with lovely fruit trees. He put two watchmen in the garden, one of them blind and the other one so lame he could hardly walk. One day the lame man said to the blind man, 'I see some beautiful fruit. Come, help me up onto your shoulders, and I will tell you the way to go.' The lame man sat on the shoulders of the blind man, and reached the fruit and they both ate it.

"After a few days, the owner of the garden came and asked, 'Who has eaten my beautiful fruit?' The lame man said, 'How could I have taken them? It would be impossible for me to

A page from the Mishnah Ketubot. The Mishnah is on top of the page. Below to the right is the commenatry of Obadiah of Bertinoro, who lived in Italy and then in Jerusalem in the 15th century. To the left is the commentary of Yomtov Lipmann Heller of Prague, of the 17th century.

41

reach them.' The blind man said, 'How can I have taken them, I who cannot see?' What did the king do? He placed the lame man on the shoulders of the blind man, and he punished them both together. Even so, God will judge man, body and soul together, as they are in life."

The Mishnah of Rabbi Judah

The great work of Judah Ha-Nasi was the editing of the Oral Law. By his time, many of the traditions had been written down. Each scholar had his own collection of ideas and opinions, laws and legends and interpretations of the Torah. Rabbi Akiva and his school had begun to organize the laws.

Judah Ha-Nasi took all this material, selected the laws and opinions that were most important or were accepted by most scholars, and arranged them in the six "Orders" of the Mishnah. The word Mishnah means "repetition" or "teaching"; now this teaching, which had been repeated or taught for centuries, was in an orderly form.

Extra writings which were not included in the Mishnah were carefully preserved. They could be studied, but finally, there was to be one collection of the Mishnah which would contain the most important interpretations of the law.

The six sections of the Mishnah deal with all phases of life, under the headings of agriculture, of Sabbath and holidays, of damages, of marriage and divorce, of rituals, and of purity. Although Aramaic was the language of most of the people, the entire work is written in the fine Hebrew that Rabbi Judah always used.

The Most Honored Rabbi

Judah Ha-Nasi was more respected than any other scholar. The saying grew up "If there are two opinions, and one is the opinion of Rabbi, that is the one to follow." So greatly was he esteemed that in the discussions of scholars he is called by the name *Rabbi,* without any other name being necessary. Sometimes, instead of the simple term Rabbi, he is called *Rabbenu Ha-Kadosh,* meaning "our holy rabbi."

Being such a respected person might have made Judah Ha-Nasi proud. Instead, he often said, "I have learned much from my teachers, more from my colleagues, and most of all from my pupils." He tried only to do what was right, saying, in answer to the question, "Which is the right course a man should choose?"—"That which honors him in his own eyes and in the eyes of his fellow men."

He guided his life by the principle, "Always keep in mind three things, and you will not do wrong: Tell yourself that there is above you an eye that sees, and an ear that hears; and that all your deeds are kept on record."

A story shows how important he felt it was to be kind and compassionate. He was ill and in pain for many years, and he blamed it on the fact that once a calf, being led to slaughter, had broken away and come to him as though for protection. Rabbi Judah had pushed the calf away and said, "Go; this is what you were created for." Afterwards, feeling sorry, he felt that he deserved punishment for his lack of sympathy for a dumb animal.

The story ends happily. Once he saw his serving-maid ready to sweep a nest of mice out of the house. He said to her, "Let them live, for it is written, 'His mercies are over all His works.'" Because this time he showed pity for dumb animals, he was forgiven, and his illness came to an end.

Death of a Beloved Leader

The last years of his life, Judah and his school were residents of the town of Tzippori, or Sepphoris. It was there that Abba and Samuel of Babylonia came to study with him. Judah was an old man by that time, having served as Patriarch for fifty years and more.

The people of Tzippori were in distress when they heard that the great man was lying ill and would probably not survive. For so many years had they depended on him as their leader and adviser, that they were almost in a state of panic. The story is told that the crowd waiting outside the home of Rabbi Judah had decided, "If anyone dares to tell us the rabbi is dead, we will kill him!"

When the moment came, Bar Kapparah, a faithful student, tore his clothes, covered his head, and came to the window. "What is it?" asked the people.

"The men of the earth and the angels of heaven have had a battle," said Bar Kapparah. "They both held on to the Ark of the Law, but the angels were stronger and have carried it off."

"What? Then Rabbi is dead?" the people shouted.

"It is you who have said it, not I," said the student.

It is said that the sound of weeping was so loud that it could be heard three miles away.

Rabbi Judah once said, speaking of a martyr. "Some win eternity after years of toil, others in one moment." This scholar, teacher and leader, through many years of devoted labor, won eternal remembrance in the hearts of his people.

SELECTIONS FROM THE MISHNAH

(These excerpts are from the tractate *Avot*, in the fourth Order, *Nezikim*. The tractate is often called *Pirke Avot*, "Chapters of the Fathers," or "Ethics of the Fathers.")

Moses received the Law from Sinai, and handed it on to Joshua, and Joshua to the elders, and the elders to the prophets, and the prophets handed it on to the men of the Great Synagogue. They said three things: Be careful in judgment, raise up many students, and make a fence around the Law.

*   *   *

Simon the Righteous was one of the last of the Great Synagogue. He used to say: By three things is the world preserved: by Torah, by service, and by deeds of loving kindness.

*   *   *

Rabbi Eliezer said: Let the honor of your neighbor be as dear to you as your own; and do not lose your temper easily; and repent one day before your death. Rabbi Joshua said: An evil eye and an evil nature and hatred of mankind can destroy their owner.

*   *   *

Rabbi Jose said: Let the property of your neighbor be as dear to you as your own; fit yourself for the study of the Law, for it is not yours by inheritance; and let all your deeds be done for the sake of heaven.

*   *   *

Rabbi Simon said: Be attentive in the reciting of the Shema *and the* Tefillah; *when you pray, ask God's mercy; and be not wicked in your own sight.*

*   *   *

Rabbi Tarfon said: The day is short and the task is great and the workers are lazy; and the wages are great, and the master is urgent. He used to say: It is not your job to finish the work, but you are not free to give up the task.

*   *   *

Ben Zoma said: Who is wise? He that learns from all men. Who is strong? He that controls his own desires. Who is rich? He who is happy with what he has. Who is honored? He who honors others.

Rav
Early Third Century

Samuel
177 - 257

What would happen if you lived in a city where there was no school? Imagine a place where the children spent no more than a year or two learning how to read and write; and where you were the only one of all your friends who wanted to study science and history and mathematics.

You might try to study by yourself. Your father and mother would help you as much as they could. Soon they would have to hire a private tutor to teach you at home. And finally, when you were old enough, you would have to leave home and go, perhaps far away, to an academy where you could really further your education.

All this happened to a boy named Samuel, who was born 1800 years ago in Babylonia, the land now called Iraq. As a young man, he was not only brighter than his friends, but more learned than his teachers.

Even before the boy was born, a great rabbi predicted that Samuel would be a leader of his people. The rabbi had asked Samuel's father, who was a silk merchant, to make him a robe. When the merchant brought him the garment, the rabbi teased him, saying, "You are a tradesman, but you also study the Law. You know that there was no contract signed between us, and legally I don't have to take this silken robe."

The merchant replied, "To me the spoken word of a scholar is more trustworthy than a legal contract."

The rabbi was pleased and said, "You are right. Those who study the Law should be the most honorable of men. Now, let me make a prophecy. Because you consider the given word so important, you shall have the good fortune of having a son who will be like the prophet Samuel, and whose word all Israel will recognize as true."

The Young Scholar

The boy, who was born soon afterwards,

Wall-painting in the synagogue of Dura Europos in Babylonia, built in the time of Samuel and uncovered by archeologists in 1932.

was named Samuel by his happy parents. While he was still a child he showed his brilliant mind and fine character.

Samuel quickly learned what all the children in his city of Nehardea learned: how to

Part of an Aramaic letter written in Palestine in Talmudic times. Most writings of such great age have crumbled to dust.

read and write Aramaic, the language he and his friends spoke everyday; how to read the Hebrew of the prayers and the Bible; and enough arithmetic to know how to buy and sell in the marketplace.

While his friends were satisfied that they had learned enough, Samuel continued to read and study. There were no printed books and no libraries, but his father was wealthy enough to own the scrolls of the Bible and even a few later writings. The boy read with love all the books of the Bible, learning of the centuries when his forefathers had lived in Palestine, had been exiled and returned, and had tried to make themselves a holy nation. Though he knew there was no longer a Temple or a king in Jerusalem, he dreamed of going back to see the land of the Bible.

Always on the Sabbath, and for some definite hours every day, Samuel's father took the time to study with him. Samuel, for his part, spent much time helping his father keep accounts, and learning about business and trade. To the marketplace the boy brought his knowledge of Jewish law.

Samuel saw that at harvest time, when there was plenty of grain, food sold cheaply and everyone could afford to buy it. Certain traders, however, bought some of the harvest and stored it till winter time, when there was little food available.

Then they would sell their stock to the hungry people at double or triple prices. Many could not afford it and nearly starved.

"This is against God's will," said Samuel. "The Torah teaches us to be fair to all God's children, including the poor. Merchants deserve reward for their work. But I feel that it would be proper, in keeping with Jewish law, for a merchant to make one-sixth profit, and no more.

"Most of all, no one should take advantage of times of famine. When I am a man and run my own business, I hope to buy extra food at

harvest time, store it in my warehouses, and sell it for the same price when people are hungry in the winter time."

Samuel's father was overjoyed at his son's love of justice. He saw that the study of Torah was making his son into a righteous and merciful man, as it should.

Then his thoughts turned to a subject that was often on his mind. "Am I doing the right thing," he worried, "bringing up such a boy in Babylonia, with no better teacher than myself?"

A modern class of teen-agers studying Talmud.

Other Studies

Soon the father and mother found more cause to worry. Their son's active mind would not let him rest; he sought knowledge everywhere. He visited travelers to learn other languages and to read any scrolls they might have brought with them from other countries; he spent many hours helping the physician of Nehardea and learning about medicine. At night, when others were sleeping, he left his warm room and went outside to study the stars.

"All knowledge is good," said the father. "Astronomy is a proper study for a young man. Seeing the great number of stars, and how they revolve in the heavens in a certain order, makes us appreciate the power of God."

Samuel's mother was not so sure. She saw that outside the gate of the courtyard her son would meet nightly with an elderly man, a stranger, dressed in the long robe and pointed hat of the priests of the Babylonians. She knew very well that he was one of those whom the Jews called star-worshippers. These were pagans, who did not believe in one God, but who prayed to the stars and called fire the most important power in the world.

Samuel became an expert astronomer. He knew where each constellation, or pattern of stars, would be at each season. He even made maps of the sky.

"I know the paths of heaven as well as the streets of Nehardea," Samuel could say. "The only ones without a regular course are the comets."

Several months had passed since Samuel had begun star-gazing with his elderly friend. It was almost dawn one summer night when the heathen priest, as they were walking homeward, took Samuel's arm and said in a low voice, "My son, my dear and best pupil, when will you see the truth and decide to worship the stars as my people do?"

"My teacher," Samuel answered gently, "I worship the one God who made everything, the earth, the heavens and the stars."

"But if you changed to my religion," the priest went on, "you would become a great leader. With your mind and your knowledge of the stars, you could be a fortune-teller and a magician. People would bring you gifts so that you would influence the stars for them."

"You know that a Jew cannot believe in fortune-telling or magic," Samuel said. "God, who controls the universe, is not to be influenced by magic words or the movements of the stars."

General view of the present remains of Babylon "The Great."

"I was afraid that you would be too stubborn to change," the old man said sadly. "You Jews are known to be stiff-necked."

From that time forth, the heathen teacher no longer waited for the boy at the gate.

"He taught me much," Samuel told his parents. "I have to be grateful to him. With my knowledge of the moon and stars I can

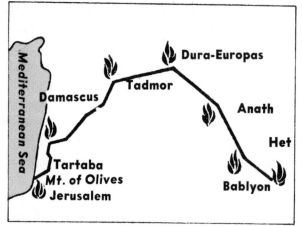

This map shows the points at which signal fires were built to announce the beginning of the new month. Starting at Jerusalem, the message was sent to the cities of Babylonia, so that all Jews would keep the holidays at the same time.

now work out the correct dates for the Jewish calendar. This will help our people in Babylonia and in Palestine to celebrate our holidays at the right time."

Samuel's father and mother looked at each other with pride. Even in this non-Jewish study, Samuel had found a way to help his people.

A Teacher Comes and Goes

Yet the parents realized more than ever that their boy must have a teacher. Samuel's father sent him for a while to study in a nearby city. When Samuel returned, his father sent letters to try to find a scholar who would live in their home and study with the boy every day.

At last the day came when the great scholar, Rabbi Levi, who had studied at the academy of Rabbi Judah Ha-Nasi in Palestine, arrived at the home of Samuel.

A new era began. Together, every day, the teacher and the pupil discussed the laws of the Torah. Samuel was strong and happy in his Jewish faith; his parents rejoiced over their son's devotion to learning.

But this happy situation did not last.

One morning Rabbi Levi, looking sadly at his pupil, said softly, "Samuel, I am very much afraid that I can't teach you Torah any longer."

"What have I done?" asked Samuel in distress. "Have I not been studying as much as I should?"

"Of course you have," answered the good rabbi, and he smiled. "It's only that I have nothing more to teach you. You know as much as I, and your mind is keener than mine."

"You have been my best teacher!" Samuel pleaded. "If you cannot teach me Torah, there is no one in the whole country who can."

Rabbi Levi nodded his head. "You're right, Samuel; there is no one left in Babylonia who can teach you Torah. I myself am leaving next week to travel to the land of our people. I am returning to the academy of Rabbi Judah Ha-Nasi."

"If only I could go there with you!" exclaimed Samuel. "But I am too young to enter the academy. The trip is long and dangerous. And could my father afford to send me?"

Abba the Tall

The day of decision finally came.

Samuel was studying at his lonely table when he heard his father call from the doorway. With his father stood a tall young stranger.

"Samuel," said the father, "I want you to meet a fine young man, the son of an old friend. His name is Abba."

Abba smiled and said, "I had to come a long way to find some one else who is serious about studying Torah."

Samuel was delighted to meet another young scholar. Abba was even more learned than he.

"There is so much I wish I could study with the great masters," said Samuel. "Nobody here can answer my questions."

"My uncle is one of the students of Rabbi Judah Ha-Nasi in Palestine," said Abba. "For a long time he has been waiting for me to come. My father is going to take me there as soon as he sells his business."

"Are you really going to the academy of Rabbi Judah?" Samuel's face was bright with joy at Abba's good fortune. Then he became thoughtful. "I hope to go too, when I'm older."

"Don't wait!" said Abba. "Rabbi Judah and the other masters are getting old. When they are gone, there may be no one left who knows the tradition as they do."

From the doorway where he had been standing, Samuel's father spoke.

"We will go up now to the Holy Land," he said. "We have waited too long as it is."

At the Academy of Judah Ha-Nasi

The trip was long and difficult, by foot, by donkey and by camel caravan, through deserts and over mountains. They thought as they traveled, "Perhaps this is the very same road Father Abraham took, from Ur to the land of Canaan."

Like all pilgrims to the land of Israel, Abba and Samuel were thrilled to step on the ground that had been trod by the men and women of the Bible. They saw, however, with sorrow, how the Jews were no longer allowed to rule their own country, and how the land was becoming waste under Roman oppression. Jews were not even allowed to visit Jerusalem to weep over the ruins of the Temple.

Only in the academy of Rabbi Judah Ha-Nasi, Judah the Prince, was there still some dignity like that of the kings and priests of old. Where the sages lived and studied, there were holiness and beauty such as had filled the Temple.

Young Samuel and his friend Abba found what they had been seeking at the academy. They discussed with their teachers the words of gentle Hillel, Rabbi Judah Ha-Nasi's ancestor, who used to say, "That which is hateful to you, do not do to another."

The two students loved to hear of Hillel, because he too had been a Babylonian who traveled to the land of Israel to study.

But it was the life of another scholar, Johanan ben Zakkai, that gave them the most to think about.

"Johanan's little school at Yavneh saved our people from forgetting the Torah when the Romans destroyed the Second Temple," said Abba. "It may be that starting a good school for the study of the Torah in Babylonia will be just as important in our day. If our people forgets its teachings, it will die out."

Samuel the Healer

Though he was younger than most of the students, Samuel soon became known to the members of the academy. It is said that he once noticed that the saintly Rabbi Judah was suffering from inflamed eyes.

"Forgive me, my teacher and rabbi," said Samuel, "but I would like to share with you some knowledge of the art of healing that

God has blessed me with." He prescribed a salve he had developed while assisting the doctor in Nehardea.

The medicine did its work well. It may have been at this time that Rabbi Judah made one of his best-known statements: "There can be much wisdom in the young, just as there may be good old wine in new bottles."

As word of the cure spread, others asked

A design in the floor of a synagogue built at Bet Alpha in the sixth century. There are signs of the zodiac, Jewish symbols, and inscriptions in Hebrew, Greek and Aramaic. This shows that the Jewish community in Palestine was still strong although Babylonia was the main center of learning.

the young man to treat them. He was usually able to help, and always gave this advice: "Preventing illness is better than waiting till we are sick and need help. We must keep our hands and faces clean, wash morning and evening, keep to a regular routine and protect ourselves from extremes in weather."

This advice, which is still good today, was very different from what many healers of that time used to say. They would prescribe magic charms to keep away illness. When he heard of such practices, Samuel became very stern. "There is no such thing as an 'evil eye,'" he taught, "and a Jew must not believe in witchcraft."

The Fair Judge

The years passed, and the two youths became mature men. Abba, the earnest scholar, stayed on in Palestine, where he became well-known under the name of Rav, meaning Master. Samuel returned to his beloved city on the banks of the Euphrates River.

The residents of the city showed their respect for his learning by asking him to be their judge. As they expected, he proved to be both kindly and just.

"One should help one's fellowman at the first sign of trouble, not wait until he is in distress," Samuel used to say. "The court of law must be like a father to orphans, protecting those who cannot help themselves."

Once a Jew and a heathen came to court, each claiming the other owed him money.

The Jew spoke to Samuel privately. "We are both Jews," he whispered. "After all, this man is a heathen, an idol worshiper. Does it matter if he gets cheated?"

The usually calm and patient Samuel became angry, and exclaimed; "It is as wrong to deceive a heathen as it is to deceive a Jew! Before the throne of God there is no difference. There are good and noble men among all the nations of the world."

Rav Founds a School

Eventually Abba also returned to Babylonia. Samuel, joined by other leaders of the Jewish community, came to greet him as Rav, the greatest Jewish scholar of the age.

The leaders of Nehardea asked Rav to become the head of the house of study in their city. Rav refused.

"My dear friend Samuel is already with

you," he said. "Samuel is a fine scholar. He loves his city and he is the one to direct your school."

Samuel became the head of the academy of Nehardea.

Rav traveled about the country as an inspector. He saw that many of the Jews, in places where there were no rabbis to teach them, had almost forgotten their religious laws. They lived, ate and drank like the heathens.

"It is my duty to teach the Jews of Babylonia to love God and the Torah, and to practice the virtues of modesty, moderation and charity," Rav decided.

In the city of Sura, Rav opened a school, one that soon became the greatest Jewish

Gateway to a Babylonian palace.

house of learning of that time. There he taught the words of the rabbis, as collected by Rabbi Judah in the Mishnah.

Not only scholars, but men who had not had much education, wished to learn from Rav. Twice a year, in the months of *Adar* (the month of *Purim*) and *Ellul* (the month before *Rosh Hashanah*) thousands of Babylonian Jews would gather in Sura to hear the master.

There was no auditorium to hold all these students, nor could they find enough room in inns or homes. So the crowd stood cheerfully outside to listen to the lectures, and at night they slept under the stars on the beach of Lake Sura.

Never since the days of Ezra, 700 years earlier, had there been such love of learning among the people.

Rav instructed his students in the way a Jew ought to act towards his neighbors.

"It is better to cast oneself into a fiery furnace," he said, "than to put one's fellow creature to shame. Whoever has no pity on his fellow is not a true Jew."

He spoke of the importance of all Jewish laws. Those who understood and obeyed the laws would be happy, Rav taught. God had made a good world for his children and wanted them to enjoy the gifts he had created for them. The laws would tell them how to live good lives, helping themselves and others.

Two Friends

Rav and Samuel remained close friends all their lives. Many were the points of law they argued and discussed together. We read in the Talmud that Rav said this, and Samuel said that.

Rav most often made the final decision. Yet Samuel's judgments were always considered worthy of respect.

An important law proclaimed by Samuel was this:

"The law of the land is the law. A Jew is not a good Jew if he disobeys the laws of the country he lives in."

As Rav and Samuel had expected, the academies of Babylonia became more important than the academies of Palestine. Like the school of Johanan ben Zakkai years before, the schools of Nehardea, of Sura, and of Pumbedita saved the Jewish people.

No longer did a Babylonian Jewish father have to worry about the education of his children. No longer did Jews need to travel to Palestine to study. Scholars came instead to the schools of Babylonia to learn and discuss the Mishnah. In time, the discussions of these later scholars were gathered together into the Gemara. The Mishnah and Gemara together make up the Talmud, the great work that the Jewish people studies to this day.

The work of Rav and Samuel and the many scholars who came after them showed the Jews how to live as good citizens, everywhere. Babylonia became for our people a second Holy Land, where Jews could live good and peaceful lives, studying and keeping the laws of the Torah, and teaching them diligently to their children.

Entrance to the underground rock tombs of the Sanhedrin in Jerusalem. Learned rabbis were entombed in stone coffins so that the people might show their respect for them through visits, study and prayer.

SELECTIONS FROM THE TALMUD (GEMARA)

The Rabbis at Yavneh used to say: "I am a creature of God and my neighbor was also created by Him; my work is in the city and his is on the farm; I rise early to my work and he rises early to his. He is not trained to do my work; but neither would I be able to do his work. You may say that I do great things and he does small things. But we know that it does not matter whether one does much or little, if only his heart is turned toward Heaven."

*　　　*　　　*

How much work Adam had to do before he had bread to eat! He ploughed, sowed, harvested, piled up the sheaves, threshed, winnowed, selected, ground the flour, kneaded and baked, and after that he ate; while I get up in the morning and find all this done for me. And how much work he had to do before he had a garment to wear! He sheared the sheep, washed the wool, combed, spun, wove, cut and sewed, and after that he had a garment to wear; while I get up in the morning and find all this done for me. How thankful we should be that we live among other men.

*　　　*　　　*

A man should always give a soft answer that turns away anger, seeking peace with his family and relatives, and with all men, even the heathen in the street, so that he may be beloved by God, and dear to his fellow men.

*　　　*　　　*

Mankind was first created as a single individual to show that we are all equal and brothers, so that the various families of men which have descended from the first man should not quarrel with each other. Since now there is so much strife although only one man was created, how much more would there be if there had been more than one!

*　　　*　　　*

A Rabbi was standing in the market place when Elijah appeared to him. The Rabbi asked him, "Is there anyone in this market place who surely deserves a share in the World to Come?" Elijah said there was none. Then two men came, travelers and poorly dressed. Elijah said, "These have a share in the World to Come." The Rabbi asked them, "What do you do?" They answered, "We are acrobats and jesters; when we see men troubled in mind we cheer them up; and when we see two men quarreling we make peace between them."

*　　　*　　　*

One who has sinned against a fellowman must say to him, "I have acted wrongly towards you." If one wrongly suspected another man, he must apologize to him and bless him. A man should always be soft as a reed, not unbending like a cedar. One Rabbi, every evening before going to bed, would pray, "Forgive anyone who has caused me trouble today."

*   *   *

The world continues to exist only for the sake of the school children. The studies of schoolchildren may not be interrupted even for the building of the Temple. A town without schools is doomed to destruction. Synagogues and houses of study are Israel's towers.

*   *   *

In Rav's days there was a teacher who was honored above all. Why? He said: "I teach children of the poor as well as of the rich; I take no fee from those who cannot afford it; and I keep a fishpond to entertain the children and keep them interested in coming to school."

UNIT TWO

THE GOLDEN AGE OF JUDAISM

The good work of Rav and Samuel, continued by their students, made Babylonia for centuries the finest Jewish community in the world. The academies of Sura, of Nehardea, and then of Pumbedita gave leadership not only to the Jews of Babylonia but also to those who lived in Egypt and North Africa, in Spain and in other countries of Europe.

The Jews of Babylonia enjoyed a good deal of freedom. There were different national and religious groups in the country, each with its own government, though all had to obey the ruling emperor. The Jews had their own leader. He was called *Resh Galuta,* the Head of the Exile, or Exilarch; for, although they were happy in Babylonia, to the Jews it was still *Galut,* or Exile. The Exilarch, supposed to be descended from the house of David, was considered almost like a king. He was the chief judge of his people, with the power to appoint other judges and officials.

Even though this was largely a good era for the Jews, there were outbreaks of war and other troubles. At times the Persian rulers of Babylonia, who were fire-worshipers, were intolerant of other religions. At one period of persecution, a Jew coud have been put to death for saying the *Shema.*

Rabina, head of the academy of Sura at that time, wanted to be sure to save the traditions of the scholars for future generations. He took the tremendous amount of material, all the commentaries on the Mishnah that had been collected by Rav Ashi of Sura a century earlier, and had them put in order.

The labors of the Tannaim, or early scholars of Palestine, resulted in the Mishnah; the discussions of the Mishnah by the Amoraim, or later scholars, became the Gemara. When their work was complete, around the year 500, the Mishnah and Gemara together made up the great Babylonian Talmud.

Illustrated Persian manuscript in Hebrew letters. The Persians ruled over Babylonia during the time of the Amoraim, and many Jews lived in all parts of the Persian empire.

THE DARK AGES BEGIN

Meanwhile, in the countries of Europe, a period had begun which is known as the Middle Ages and has also often been called the Dark Ages. The mighty Roman Empire, which had ruled over Palestine and had controlled so much of the world, had come to an end. Invasions, rebellions and civil wars had sapped the strength of Rome; injustice and luxury had weakened its people. The legions withdrew and taxes were no longer paid to Rome.

Europe was not under one rule, but was broken up into little kingdoms and dukedoms. The Christian religion, which had spread over Europe, was a strong force. The leaders of the church were often the only ones who could read or write. They taught the people and had great influence on the kings and noblemen.

The eastern Empire of Byzantium took over from Rome the rule of Palestine. These Christian rulers tried to destroy Jewish life by making it more and more difficult for Jews to build synagogues or keep their religion. Nonetheless, the oppressed people were faithful to the Commandments, and continued their studies.

In addition to the Palestinian Talmud, the scholars of Palestine produced other valuable literature. The *Midrashim,* interpretations of events and sayings found in the Bible, were collected in Palestine. These works are a treasure-house of fascinating legends and lessons that can be learned from the lives of the people of the Bible.

As the community in Palestine became smaller and suffered more persecutions, the Jews withdrew to certain towns such as Safed, and there continued to devote themselves to study.

A page from a Midrash copied in Constantinople in 1620. It tells the sad story of the sages who were put to death by the order of Hadrian.

MOHAMMED AND ISLAM

It has been said that Judaism is the mother religion, and from the mother came two daughters, Christianity and Islam. Both daughter faiths based themselves on the Jewish Bible and the Jewish concept of one God. Christianity was already the major religion of Europe and the Byzantine Empire, when, in the seventh century, the new religion of Islam was born.

Mohammed, the prophet of Islam, was an Arab camel driver of the city of Mecca, where many idols were worshiped. He was uneducated and grew up as a pagan, but, like many Arabs, he was much impressed by what he had heard of the teachings of the Jews. He had visions which told him to proclaim the existence of one God, Allah, creator of the world and of man; and which persuaded him that he, Mohammed, was the prophet of Allah.

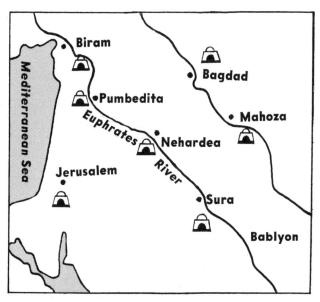

On this map of Babylonia, you may find the cities of Pumbedita, Nehardea and Sura along the Euphrates River; and, to the east, Mahoza and Bagdad.

At first, Mohammed hoped that the Jews would follow him, for, like them, he insisted that God was one and not to be divided, and could never appear in human form. He included some of the Bible figures, such as Abraham and Moses, in his "Bible," the *Koran;* and said the Arabs were descended from Abraham's son Ishmael. The Jews, however, did not respect him, and made fun of his ignorance. Mohammed turned against them and became their enemy.

For some years, Mohammed gained few followers. He was persecuted by pagan Arab priests and forced to flee (622). At this point, he decided that in order to spread his religion he had the right to attack unbelievers and use any means of warfare against them. Very swiftly, his band of warlike followers increased, and he was able to spread Islam throughout all of Arabia.

The armies of Islam conquered one country after another. North Africa and Egypt and most of Palestine came under their sway. In Europe itself, most of Spain was in Moslem hands.

Babylonia and the whole Persian empire soon fell. Although the new rulers restricted the rights of Jews and other unbelievers, they did not interfere very much in their community life. The Exilarch continued to govern the Jews, now subject to the Caliph of Bagdad.

The heads of the academies continued to teach their students. These leaders of the schools of Pumbedita and of Sura were considered so great that they were called by the name *Gaon,* the Hebrew word meaning Excellency or Glory. The *Geonim* received letters asking questions on Jewish law from all parts of the world. Their answers, or *Re-*

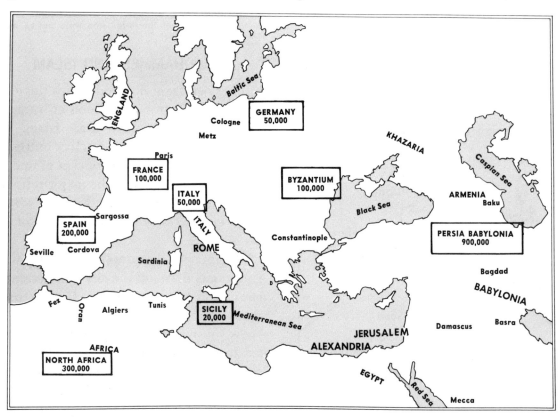

Centers of Jewish population in Christian and Moslem countries in the years 640 to 1100. The largest number, 900,000, lived in Persia-Babylonia, to the east, which after 640 came under Moslem rule. The large communities of Spain (200,000) and North Africa (300,000) were also under Moslem rule. Christian lands shown are France, Germany, Italy, and Byzantium.

Karaites living in the Crimea, part of Russia. They were treated by the government as being of a different religion than the Jews.

sponsa, were eagerly received and carefully preserved.

THE KARAITES

The Jews of Babylonia lived their daily lives not according to the law of the Caliph or the Exilarch, but according to Jewish law as presented in the Talmud, and as further explained by the Geonim. There were some who rebelled against the authority of the Talmud and the teachers of the law.

Anan ben David, a learned Jew of Bagdad, spoke against the Geonim and the rabbis (760). He was imprisoned by the Caliph, but escaped and fled to Palestine. There he founded a group, a religious sect, called the Karaites, or *B'nai Mikra.* (*Mikra* means the reading, or the Bible.) The Karaites wanted to keep the laws only as stated in the Torah, and to disregard the many laws and customs which had grown up among the Jews and which were described in the Talmud.

The Karaites were supposed to study the Bible text for themselves and to follow it as they thought they should. There were for some time many different ideas among them, until leaders arose who explained the law. Thus there developed a Karaite interpretation of the laws; for it was impossible to obey the laws of the Torah without some interpretation.

Karaite law was not easier to live by than Talmudic law. Many of the prayers and some laws of *Kashrut,* or dietary laws, were set aside. Other laws, however, such as those concerning marriage, medicine, and clothing, were made much more strict.

There was strong disagreement between the Karaites and the traditional Jews, whom they called *Rabbanites,* because they followed the teachings of the rabbis. The schools of Babylonia of course remained "Rabbanite," as did the majority of the Jews of the world. The claim of the Karaites, however, that theirs was the true interpretation of Jewish law, had to be answered. The people looked to the Geonim to answer questions which the Karaites and the Moslems raised about the Jewish religion.

The greatest Gaon was Saadia (882-942), who came from Egypt to head the academy of Sura in the year 928. He answered the Karaites, and helped the Jews to understand their own tradition by translating the Bible into Arabic. His greatest work, the *Book of Beliefs and Doctrines,* explained Jewish ideas in a logical way. He not only looked at the words of the Bible and Talmud, but used his own mind and the methods of the Moslem philosophers, the greatest thinkers of that time. Saadia made the study of Jewish ideas scientific.

The earliest inscription concerning Jews in France, a grave-stone from the city of Narbonne dated 688. For some time, Narbonne was a center of Jewish learning.

Following Saadia's death, there were periods of persecution in Babylonia. The school at Sura closed. There were two outstanding Geonim at Pumbedita, Sherira and Hai; but when Hai was put out of office by the Caliph, the worldwide influence of the Babylonian Jewish community came to an end.

THE FOUR SCHOLARS

There is a story of four scholars of Babylonia who set out by ship to visit other Jewish communities and collect money for the support of the academy. They never returned to Babylonia, for their ship was captured by pirates, and the rabbis were taken prisoner.

The pirate captain wanted to sell his captives as slaves. He knew that the Jews would pay a large ransom to rescue one of their brothers. He sold Rabbi Shemariah in Alexandria, Egypt; the Jews recognized him as a scholar and he became head of a school in Cairo. The Jews of the North African coast redeemed Rabbi Hushiel, who became head of a school in Kairuan. Rabbi Nathan, the third scholar, arrived at the French city of Narbonne, and taught there.

Dressed in the poor clothes of a slave, and unrecognized by anyone, Rabbi Moses and his little son Enoch were ransomed by Jews of Cordova, in Spain. The story tells that Moses made his way to the school, and stood silently in the back of the room while the students discussed a passage in the Talmud. The students kept making the same mistake, until Rabbi Moses gently corrected them. They listened in amazement to the brilliant explanation of the ragged stranger.

The president of the school then stepped down and said, "I am no longer your rabbi and judge; but this man, who is clothed in sackcloth, is my teacher, and I am his pupil." The congregation appointed Rabbi Moses their judge and teacher, provided him with fine clothes, and paid honor to him. From that time Cordova became a leading city of learning among the Jews.

This dramatic story is an explanation of

Costumes of German Jews in the 13th century. Jews were required by law to wear pointed hats, so that everyone could know who they were.

how Jewish authority and learning left Babylonia and came to the other countries where Jews lived. For it is clear that around the year 1000, the communities of North Africa, Egypt, Spain and France had grown more important, and the Jews of these lands no longer supported the academies of Babylonia or sent their questions to that country.

AMONG THE CHRISTIANS

The Jews of the Rhineland and in other French or Germanic communities found themselves living among Christians. The Church was a powerful force all during the Middle Ages. When Europe was divided into small areas, each with its own ruler, the Church was the only unifying influence.

The leaders of the Christian Church believed theirs was the only religion. They fought against the Moslems and tried to convert the pagans and also the Jews to Christianity. There were many harsh decrees against the Jews: they could not own land, or live outside certain areas, or enter many trades. In times of more severe persecution, Jews were forced to convert or pay with their lives.

The worst era for the Jews was the time of the Crusades (beginning 1096). The Church aroused the people of Europe to join a great march to the Holy Land, Palestine, in order to drive the "infidel" Moslems from Jerusalem.

The Crusaders did not wait till they reached Jerusalem, where indeed many of them never arrived, to attack the "infidel." The men of the Frst Crusade destroyed whole communities of Jews in the Rhineland. In this and later Crusades, Jewish property was taken away, and Jews were told to become Christian or be killed. Sometimes, leaders of the Church tried to stop this robbery and murder. But the masses of the people used the excuse of religion to attack, plunder and kill the unfortunate Jews.

The first Hebrew book to appear in print was Rashi's commentary on the Torah, printed in Italy, 1475. This type face became known as "Rashi script."

LIGHTS IN THE EXILE

All through the centuries, however, there were Jewish communities where families lived and worked, and where education continued. In Mayence, Rabbenu Gershom (960-1028) taught the Talmud so well that his pupils from Germany and Italy called him "The Light of the Exile."

The great Solomon ben Isaac, known as Rashi (1040-1105), studied at the school of Mayence and other schools as well. His wonderfully clear Hebrew commentaries on Bible and Talmud made him the best-known and most beloved of scholars. His saintly character was known to all. Living through the time of the First Crusade, Rashi was merciful enough to give the opinion that Jews who had been forced to convert should be forgiven and welcomed back to their people.

Rashi's family carried on the scholarly tradition he had started. His grandsons Isaac, Samuel and Jacob ben Meir called their own writings *Tosafot*, Additions. Their group is called the school of the Tosafists. Jacob was known as Rabbenu Tam, a beloved leader who encouraged the Jews and helped unify them.

An inscription in stone from a medieval synagogue of Cordova, Spain.

THE GOLDEN AGE IN SPAIN

The Jews who lived under Moslem rule were more fortunate, as a whole, than those who lived under Christian rule. There were outbreaks of intolerance, but for centuries Jews of Moslem countries, particularly Spain, were able to live in peace and to gain wealth and culture.

Spain flourished under the Moslems. Fine cities and great courts were built up; trade prospered. The rulers loved learning, most especially Aristotle's philosophy, and other wisdom of the ancient Greeks, which was translated into Arabic. Mathematics, astronomy and medicine were studied, and honor was given to the arts of song, poetry, and architecture.

Jews were able to share in this great civilization not only as skilled physicians, writers and translators, but even as leading business men and statesmen. Hasdai ibn Shaprut (915-970), physician and poet, became chief adviser and vizier in the court of the Caliph of Cordova. He founded the Spanish academy for study of the Talmud, which Rabbi Moses came to head; and used his wealth and influence to help men of learning.

In the Spanish province of Granada, another learned Jew, Samuel ibn Nagdela, was vizier to two rulers and was also called *Nagid,* or Prince of the Jewish community. Samuel Ha-Nagid, like Hasdai, held the highest position in his country's government and at the same time gave religious leadership in his own Jewish community. Such learned Jewish statesmen were not found except in Spain during this "Golden Age."

Like their Moslem neighbors, the Jews of Spain loved poetry and philosophy. Solomon ibn Gabirol (1021-1070) was a poet and a philosopher, who wrote his ideas in the form of a conversation, or dialogue, between a teacher and a pupil. His book, *The Fountain of Life,* was prized by Christian and

תדע   והשב־ל כי על כל דבור ודבור של זה הספר מטפלים ו
ומתגלגלים ומתכפלים להתגולל ולהתחבר אליהם ז
בחכמה אגדות ומדרשים וראיות וטעמים מן הפסוק ומן התלכ־וד
כי לא יצא מפי חכמי אומות העולם דבר אמתי שלא יהא נרמז ב
בתורתנו אך לא חפצתי להאריך ואפרשנו לפי משמעות פשוטו ב
בקוצר לשון לפי מעט קט שכלי כאשר הראו לי מן השמים כי לא
היה לי בזה הפירוש רב וחבר ··

זה ספר מבחר הפנינים

במליצת החכמי׳ ה,רמוני׳ומשל׳ פלוספוסים הראשונים ומוסרם
ומצותם ודבריהם וחידותם בכל ענין שאדם צריך אליו בחכמה
וביראה ובמוסר ובדרך ארץ מסודר לשערים ב־כל ענינים ··
פירוש
זה   ספר מבחר הפנינים במליצתהו…מים הקדמונים וכו׳ פי׳ זה ספר
מבחר נקרא מבחר הפנינים לפי שכן מבחר החכמה שכ׳ יקרה היא
הפנינים : במליצת,כלומ׳ מוצא ונחב ב הוא זה הספר במליצות חכמים ה
הקדמונים׳ שהביננו ופירשו דברי מ,שלי׳ של חכמה שמשלו הם הפלוספוסי׳
הראשונים : המשל הוא הדונא וסתרון המשל תמועתנו נקרא מליצה כ
כמה דאת אמר להבין משל ומליצה כו׳ : פלוספוסים הם חכמי הישמעאלי
נגלחי אדם קורים להם פלוסופים שמספרי חכמי הישמעאלים הכתובים
בלשון ערב נעתק זה הספר והעתקו והועתק ,ו ,והחלף ללשון הקרש בדמ,ין לשון ז
ערב: לפיכך תמצא לשונכנו כבד בזה הספר בכמה מקומות׳ : ומוסרם ות
ומצותם כו׳ כלומ׳ בזה הספר תמצא מוסרם ומצותם של חכמי הקדמוני׳
:ודבריהם וחדותם אשר השכילו בכל ענין שארם צריך להם הן בחכמה ו

A page from the book "Choice of Pearls," a collection of philosophic writings by Solomon Ibn Gabirol.

A letter in Hebrew from a Khazar Jew, dated 950. In this letter are recounted the incidents that led to the conversion of the Khazars to Judaism and events that took place in Khazaria during the 10th century.

book, the *Kuzari*. This work explains the wisdom of Judaism through dialogues, which Judah Ha-Levi imagined, between King Bulan of the Khazars and the rabbi who taught him about the Jewish faith.

The greatest mind of all was Moses Maimonides (1135-1205), called the Rambam. He, too, although persecution made him leave his home and settle for the latter part of his life in Egypt, was a product of Spain, born in Cordova.

Maimonides, in his works of genius, clarified the Mishnah, provided a complete code of laws for the Jews in the *Mishneh Torah,* and explained the philosophy of Judaism in the finest and highest terms in the *Guide for the Perplexed.*

Maimonides was forced to hide his faith and to change his home many times because of Moslem persecution; yet he became an honored citizen of Cairo, chief physician to

Moslem readers. Students are grateful to other brilliant philosophers of his time, such as Abraham ibn David who recorded Jewish history, and Abraham ibn Ezra, keen commentator on the Bible.

There were many other outstanding writers, thinkers and poets during this period. The most loved and respected of the poetic philosophers of Spain was Judah Ha-Levi (1086-1145), who was, like many Jews of his time, a skilled physician and a man of science as well as a master of the Arabic language. His poems, whether on love, on nature, on God or on Zion, are marked by tender feeling beautifully expressed.

Judah Ha-Levi used the well-known historical fact of the conversion of the powerful pagan tribe, the Khazars, to Judaism about 400 years before his time, as the basis for his

The gravestone of a grandson of Moses Maimonides, found in Cairo, Egypt. Because of the greatness of the Rambam, the inscription reads: This is the grave of David, grandson of Rabbenu the Gaon Moses ben Maimon, Light of the Exile."

the Sultan, and a famous figure throughout the Arab world.

The eight centuries following the fall of the Roman Empire (about the year 500) are often called the Dark Ages by general historians. This same period, which saw the center of Jewish life shift from Babylonia to Moslem Spain, and to Christian Europe, can be called Dark Ages for the Jews; for there was much persecution and bloodshed.

However, because of the magnificent work of the heroic scholars of this time, of Saadia in Babylonia, of Rashi in France, of the many great men of Spain, crowned by Moses Maimonides—because of their wonderful contribution to law and learning and hope, this time can truly be called a Golden Age for the Jewish people.

Saadia Gaon

882 - 942

In his conference chamber, surrounded by his advisers, the Exilarch, leader of the Jews of Babylonia, sat forward in his throne-like chair.

"If only we lived in the time of Rav!" he exclaimed. "Ah, that was the time of great rabbis and teachers. Then we would have had no problem in finding the right man."

"You are right, honored David ben Zakkai," said the scholar Joseph ben Jacob. "In the old days there were real leaders. Now we are all unworthy. Not a man in Babylonia is wise enough to deserve the title of Gaon of Sura."

For it seemed that the school at Sura, founded 700 years before by Rav, could go on no longer. There was no one to head the great center of Jewish learning, to which students had come for centuries from all parts of the world. Gaon, meaning Excellency, was a title not easily won.

"There is only one solution," said another adviser with some hesitation. "There is a fine school at Pumbedita, almost as old as the one at Sura. We must admit that the high standards of Sura have been going down. Why not

A bowl engraved with Hebrew writing, found in Babylonia.

close the school of Sura and be satisfied with one academy for the whole country?"

All looked at David ben Zakkai. But before the Exilarch could speak, a young man stepped forward and raised pleading hands towards him. "Father, don't listen to this counsel of despair," said young Judah. "You can't let the academy of Sura close its doors. Forever after, people will say you allowed the glory of Jewish learning to die out."

The Blind Adviser

Those standing near the Exilarch made way with respect as an old man with a cane felt his way forward.

"Speak, Nissim," said the Exilarch. "We want to hear the advice of our most venerable scholar."

"I am blind, but I have seen much in my lifetime," said Nissim. "Your son is right. You cannot close the school. Never before have our people needed teachers more than now. They are confused and do not know what to believe.

"Many of them listen to the teachings of the Moslems. Some are Karaites, who do not obey the laws of the Talmud, but make themselves different from their brothers. Our people need a new leader to guide them."

"You are a man of many years and much wisdom," David ben Zakkai said. "Would you be willing to become the Gaon of Sura?"

Nissim smiled sadly. "You are kind to show me so much honor," he said. "But I am too old, and too tired. You must find a young and vigorous man."

"Then you must advise me," said David. "We must find a young scholar who knows both Bible and Talmud. He must also know languages, science and philosophy, so that he can find answers to all arguments against our faith. He must be a writer and teacher, and, above all, a faithful Jew. Can you find me such a man?"

Synagogue of the Karaites in Jerusalem.

"There is only one such man," answered Nissim.

"Who is he?" asked David eagerly.

"Saadia ben Joseph, the young genius from Egypt, who brightened our lecture-halls a few years ago."

"Saadia!" exclaimed David. "A genius, no doubt of that. But he's a stranger, a foreigner. How would he act? Would he know what we expect of him?"

"You have asked my advice," said Nissim. "Our generation may not be the generation of Rav, but it is blessed with one great light. This young man Saadia has already written works that outshine anything of the past hundred years. If we can get him to come to Sura, foreigner or no, we can count ourselves blessed."

Whispering arose among the advisers. Some shook their heads; others nodded in agreement.

"There is one other thing," said Nissim. "Saadia is known to be strong-minded and independent. He will fight for what he believes is right and will never give in."

David frowned. "I don't want a man who will always be arguing with everyone. He might even quarrel with me!"

His son Judah spoke up. "I would like my father to be remembered as the man who appointed the greatest Gaon of all time, and restored the glory of Torah to Sura."

"We have decided," said David. "I will invite Saadia to become the Gaon. In case of any trouble, I, the Exilarch, will be able to keep him in his place."

Saadia the Teacher

There was excitement in the academy at the news that Saadia of Egypt was to become the Gaon of Sura. All the students remembered the serious young man, who hardly ever smiled, but spent all his time at work and study. Some exchanged copies of prayers and of Hebrew poetry he had written; others spoke of his dictionary and his Arabic translations of Hebrew works.

Hundreds awaited his coming in the court of study. The oldest and most learned men, seated on benches in the front seven rows, stood up as the new Gaon came in and took his place before them.

Saadia was not a man to waste time in idle talk. "We begin study of the order of *Mo'ed* (Festivals), the first section, *Shabbat*," he announced.

Some of the students turned to look at each other. They were glad that Saadia had chosen this section of the Talmud. They listened intently and joined in the discussion on how to keep the Sabbath holy.

After some hours, Saadia signaled that he wished to address the group. "There are those who say," he began, "that the rabbis of the Talmud have made the Sabbath hard to observe, with their listing of so many laws and principles.

"But the Karaites, who try to follow the Bible without learning what the Talmud teaches, have changed our Sabbath of joy into a dark and lonely day.

"The Karaites read in the Bible that one may not light fire in his home on the Sabbath, so they sit without warmth or light, and eat cold food. They do not go out of their homes on the Sabbath, because of another mistake they make in reading the Bible.

"The rabbis of Palestine and Babylonia, however, knew the true meaning of the words of the Torah. Although one may not kindle a fire or cook on the Sabbath, one may leave a light burning, so that the Sabbath may be a day of light.

"And the rabbis explain that although one may not make a journey on the Sabbath, or go out to weekday activities, one may leave one's home to attend services, or visit, or take a walk.

"The rabbis of the Talmud did not make up new, extra laws for the Jews to follow. The people themselves were already living according to both the Torah, which is the Written Law, and the Oral or Unwritten Law. The rabbis interpreted the laws, showing how all tradition was based on the Torah, and tried to help the Jews live by the law. The Talmud and the life of the Jews are bound together."

"How wisely he shows us the errors of the Karaites," young Judah said to his father, the Exilarch. "This man will unite all Israel again in loyalty to our tradition."

New Glory to Sura

Saadia's fame spread. New teachers and new students came from Egypt, from North Africa, even from Spain. Travelers brought letters to Saadia, asking for help and advice.

"We know the Torah is holy and true," wrote one rabbi. "But we also know, and must believe, that God is a spirit and has no bodily form like a human being.

"What can we believe when the Bible speaks of 'the hand of God' or 'the strong arm of God'; or says that 'God looked down' or 'God came' as though He were a person?"

Saadia answered this question. "Of course we do not believe that God has a hand, or is in any way like a human being. But how else can you explain the power of God? People cannot imagine what God is like, or how He carries out His will. The Bible had to use words that people would understand."

The months of *Kallah*, the two months of the year when Jews gathered from all over the country to study in Sura, again became important. Once more, as in the days of Rav, the delight of studying the Torah filled the hearts of the Jewish people.

David the Exilarch was pleased and proud. "The man I appointed has brought back Sura's ancient glory," he boasted.

Saadia Stands Firm

Now that the Exilarch, the Head of the Exile, did not have to worry about the schools, he could give more time to acting as judge for the Jews under his authority.

A difficult case came up in court. David had to decide who was the owner of some valuable property. He wrote out his decision and handed it to his son Judah, saying: "Take my decision to the Gaon of Pumbedita and the Gaon of Sura, and ask them to sign it. If these two wise scholars agree with my judgment, no one will dare to criticize me."

Judah traveled to Pumbedita and obtained the signature of its Gaon. Then he went to Sura.

Saadia received him pleasantly and asked what was his request. Judah gave him the document.

Saadia studied it carefully for some time, and then gave it back. "I cannot sign this document," he said firmly, "because I do not agree with your father's decision."

With some fear, Judah returned to his father's court. David became very angry.

"I am the Exilarch! I am almost as great as the Caliph of this country, and I must be obeyed. I appointed Saadia to Sura, and I can depose him any time I choose. Take this back to him and tell him I insist that he sign it."

Judah returned unhappily to Sura. Saadia again welcomed him. "What is troubling you?" he asked.

"This same document," said Judah. "My father insists that you sign it."

Saadia shook his head. "I cannot."

"You are creating trouble," said Judah. "For the sake of peace, and for your own sake, you had better sign."

"I cannot go against the Torah," said Saadia. "Is it not written, 'You shall not respect persons in judgment!' This judgment is not fair; it shows special favor to a rich man. I will not sign."

"We were warned about your wilfulness!" Judah exclaimed. "You should never have been made Gaon of Sura!"

"I will discuss it no further," said Saadia firmly. He called his servant to show Judah out of the house.

Exile From Sura

David the Exilarch walked up and down in his chamber, shaking his fist. Secretly, he felt ashamed of himself; but this made him all the more furious. Finally he announced to his officers:

"Saadia is no longer Gaon. He may never again set foot in the academy. He and his family must leave Sura at once!"

The advisers were afraid to argue with their angry leader, but one asked gently, "Then who will be Gaon of Sura?"

"I don't care who, as long as it isn't the stubborn Saadia!" David raged. "Let it be Joseph ben Jacob. He's a teacher, too, and a quiet man who doesn't make trouble."

Dismay fell upon Saadia and his many admirers at this harsh action. But there were those who agreed with David. The Caliph, the Moslem ruler of the whole country, announced that the word of the Exilarch must be obeyed, and decreed that Saadia would have to leave Sura.

Just two years after coming to Sura, Saadia sadly left the academy and went to live in Bagdad.

Saadia's Greatest Work

Unhappy and in poor health, Saadia remained a fighter for justice. He wrote a defense of himself which convinced most of the Jews of Babylonia that he was right. Yet he could not return to Sura, as long as David would not allow it.

"I cannot meet with my students," Saadia mourned. "But I must keep on doing the work God has assigned me. I will continue to teach through my writings."

Day after day, and often far into the night, Saadia labored. Because of his travels in different countries, and the many letters he had received, he knew what the Jews of his time needed and what questions they wanted answered.

He knew the people longed for a book of prayers, so he compiled a *Siddur*. This included the *Shema* and the *Amidah* which all the Jews of the world said, and other prayers for weekdays, Sabbath and holidays. He included many of his own poetic prayers as well.

He translated the entire Bible into Arabic, for there were many Jews who did not know Hebrew well. Living in Arabic-speaking countries, they were more familiar with that language than with their holy tongue.

To each of his books Saadia added explanations, answers to questions that a reader might ask. Studying one of Saadia's books was almost like sitting in a classroom with him as teacher.

In his most important work, Saadia explained the thoughts and ideas of the Jewish religion about God, man, and the world. *The Book of Beliefs and Doctrines* was written by Saadia Gaon in Arabic; when it was translated into Hebrew, so that Jewish scholars living anywhere in the world might understand it, it was called *Sefer Emunot v'Deot*.

At all times there have been wise men who tried to understand and explain the world and the men who live in it. These men are called philosophers. The philosophers of Saadia's time were saying that one ought to figure out the truth in one's own mind, rather than read books like the Bible to find out God's will.

The main idea in Saadia's book is that the Bible and man's reason agree. If a man follows what his own mind tells him, he will come to the same ideas as those of the Bible.

Saadia felt that a thinking person would surely believe that God is One and that He created the entire universe; that man has free will to follow God's law, and that if he does he will be rewarded; that the soul of man does not die, but is eternal; and that the righteous will be redeemed.

God gave the Torah to the world, said Saadia, because man thinks slowly and can make mistakes; it would take him too long to figure out the truth by himself.

Saadia helped those in his day who were worried that "modern science" contradicted the teachings of Judaism.

A title-page of *Sefer Emunot v'Deot.*

The Exilarch Yields

Meanwhile, the quarrel over Saadia still distressed the Jews of Babylonia. Leaders demanded his return to Sura. "The glory of our generation sits in Bagdad," they said. "Sura is like a desert."

Finally, after seven years, one of his advisers appealed to David in the presence of a large group of Jewish leaders. "How long will you continue to hold a grudge? Strife is a sin and leads only to evil. Show your own greatness, and make peace with Saadia."

David himself had felt remorse for a long time for what he had done. "Send for Saadia," he said. "Let him return."

Friendship Renewed

The Exilarch sat in his chamber, waiting for Saadia. A large crowd watched anxiously. They knew David's bad temper; they also knew Saadia's stubbornness. They did not know what would happen when the two met face to face.

Saadia and his supporters entered the chamber. Though he was not old, the scholar looked worn and weary. His back was bent from years of writing; his fingers were gnarled from holding the quill.

David arose from his chair, descended from the platform, and walked toward the scholar. Saadia, the stern, fearless man, walked toward the Exilarch.

The two met and embraced like long-lost brothers.

Tears of joy were in the eyes of the onlookers. They were happy that David, their leader, had finally placed the good of his people above his own pride. They saw, too, that Saadia was willing to forgive the injustice that had been done to him.

Saadia spent the holiday of Purim at the home of the Exilarch. He then returned to Sura among rejoicing students.

The two strong men were now friends. When the Exilarch died, and when his son Judah soon after also passed away, Saadia adopted David's orphaned grandson as his own child.

Thus a sad quarrel ended. But some good had come of it. If Saadia had stayed at Sura all the while, he would not have had the time to write the books he completed in Bagdad. He became a teacher not only to the students of Sura, but to all the Jews of the world.

Saadia could have been describing himself when he wrote: "God does not leave His people at any time without a scholar whom He inspires; so that he may in turn teach the people, and make them better."

SELECTIONS FROM SAADIA GAON

Many people have gone astray and failed to gain wisdom. Some of them do not know which road to take; and others take the right road, but do not travel far enough.

* * *

There are four roots of knowledge. We can find things out by (1) Sense perception, that which we see or hear; (2) Reason, that which we figure out in our minds; (3) Inference, judging one fact from another (such as that there must be fire if we see smoke); and (4) Tradition, that which is written down or remembered.

* * *

Some of the ignorant people in our nation think that the eclipse of the moon occurs when a dragon swallows the moon. Surely God wants us to inquire and seek out knowledge, in addition to accepting tradition.

* * *

There are those who believe in two eternal agents, one good and one evil, one of light and one of darkness. God is the only agent. There is no principle of darkness; darkness is only the absence of light. If a man stands in the sun and puts the palms of his hands one upon the other like a dome, the space between them will be dark. He shuts out the light and thus causes darkness, because the light is absent. Similarly, evil is the absence of good; and occurs through the free will of man.

* * *

Since God is the Creator, He must have life, power and wisdom. He is eternal, all powerful, and all wise; though in a way we cannot understand. Obviously, ordinary words cannot really describe God. We use ordinary words, such as "God was kind" or "God was angry" to fit our own understanding.

* * *

The Bible includes a record of the past intended to instruct us in the right way of obedience towards Him. Instruction for a good life needs three things: (1) a list of commandments; (2) reward and punishment which follow; (3) an account of those who gave good service and prospered, as well as of those who did wrong and perished. Let me give an illustration: A man visits a sick person afflicted with fever. Now if he tells him not to eat meat or drink wine, he has already done something to instruct him in the right way, but not enough. If he tells him, "otherwise you will get pleurisy," he has told him of the punishment for disobeying the instruction. It still is not complete until he gives him the example "as was the case with X who contracted pleurisy." Thus he has given instruction, warning, and example, as th Bible does.

Every Jew must study the Torah, whether he is poor or rich, healthy or ailing, young or old. None of the laws equals the study of the Torah in importance; Torah is above all the laws, because it leads to fulfilling all of them. Knowledge of the Torah cannot be reached by those who are lazy or by those who study in the midst of revelry.

*   *   *

A teacher should not be angry or excited when his pupils cannot understand a subject. He should go over it with them many times until they understand. A pupil should not be afraid to ask questions. If a teacher loses patience, the pupil may say to him: "Master, this is the Torah! I must learn it even though I am not very smart."

*   *   *

Men are different one from another. Some are always angry, while others are always quiet. Some are too proud, and some too meek. Some are greedy and want everything; others do not even desire what they should have. A man should be neither easily angered nor always composed. He should not close his hand, nor should he be too lavish. He should be neither hilarious nor gloomy. He who avoids extremes and follows the middle course in all things is a wise man.

Rashi

1040 - 1105

It was early morning in the month of June in the French town of Troyes. The sun had just risen and the air was cool, as a father and his two daughters walked briskly down the cobblestone street that led to the edge of town.

A farmer, leading a very small donkey, who in turn pulled a rough cart laden with turnips, touched his hand to his cap.

"Good morning, Rabbi Solomon," he said. "Good morning, little daughters. You are out to the vineyards early today."

"The grapes will be showing soon, Master Pierre," said the father. "It's time to trim and tie the vines."

"And we're going to help him!" said Miriam, the older of the two girls.

The farmer shook his head. "It's too bad you have to do this kind of work, Rabbi Solomon," he said.

Solomon ben Isaac smiled. "Why is it bad, Master Pierre?" he asked gently. "Doesn't it say in our Bible, yours as well as mine, that by the sweat of his brow man shall earn his bread?"

"But you, Rabbi Solomon, you are a great man, a scholar, who knows the meaning of the word of God," Pierre insisted," You should spend your time talking to angels, not working with your hands."

"Work is a blessing, not a disgrace," said Solomon ben Isaac. "One of our greatest teachers was a woodchopper, and one was a shoemaker. You and I should both be glad we are doing honest work on God's good earth."

Pierre nodded happily and wished them good day. He did not hear Miriam saying to her father as they walked away, "But Papa, it would be nicer for you, wouldn't it, if you had more time for studying and writing? I woke up last night and saw your candle burning when everyone else was asleep."

"I can both work and write," answered her

Title-page of Rashi's commentary on the Pentateuch, published by Elijah Aboab, (Amsterdam, 17th century).

father, "as long as God gives me strength, and a good wife and good daughters to help me."

The Young Student

Pierre had just turned another corner, followed by his patient donkey, when he met another early riser. This was a young man of about fifteen, dressed in heavy clothes and walking-boots, and carrying a traveler's staff.

"Excuse me, Master," the young man began. "I have just come into town. Can you tell me the way to the house of Rashi?"

"I don't know the name Rashi," said Pierre. "But you're a stranger; you're a polite gentleman; and you're not going to the market, because you're not carrying anything to sell. You must be looking for Rabbi Solomon."

"Yes, I am," said the young man eagerly.

"I called him Rashi because that's what my father calls him: the first letters of his name, Rabbi Shlomo Izhaki. Can you tell me where he lives?"

"Just around the corner and the last house on the road," said Pierre. "He's not home, but I'm sure they'll make you welcome. All students are welcome there."

"How did you know I was a student?" asked the young man.

"Who else would come so far, as I can tell by the dust on your boots, to see the Rabbi?" said Pierre. "Good luck and good day to you. Get along there, Suzette." And Pierre, donkey and cart set off to the market.

Rashi's Daughter

The young man knocked at the heavy wooden door before him. He felt his heart beating strongly. Soon he would meet the great Rashi!

The door opened. There stood a ten-year-old girl, with a white cloth tied around her long hair, and a broom made of twigs in her hand.

"Good day," she said brightly, and waited.

"Good day," said the young man. "I'm Meir ben Samuel. I've come from Rameru. I have a letter here from my father."

"I'm Jochebed. I live right here. I'm sweeping today, because my sisters went out to the vineyards. Let me see the letter."

Meir ben Samuel laughed and held the letter high above Jochebed's head. "You're not very respectful to your elders, are you? Why should I give you the letter? You couldn't read a word."

Jochebed's mouth opened wide. "What do you mean?" she exclaimed angrily. "Do you think that the daughters of Rashi can't read? Just because we're girls? I even dry his pages for him with sand, and put them in order, and I'm the first one to read them. I can read French and Hebrew both!"

She turned to go back into the house. Meir followed her meekly. "I'm sorry," he pleaded. "I don't know many girls who can read, especially ones as young as you."

"I'm not so young," said Jochebed, still angry. "I'm almost eleven. Mama, here's a student who came with a letter for Papa."

Meir was glad to turn from the indignant girl to her kind and thoughtful mother, who immediately offered him a warm breakfast.

"I want you to feel as though you were my own son," she said. "I remember how hard it was for my husband, all through his youthful years, when he went from town to town to study. How often he went hungry! How many nights did he sleep on a stone floor, so as to be near his great teachers!"

"I would gladly sleep on a stone floor, to study with the greatest teacher of all," said Meir.

A page with Rashi's commentary.

Jochebed, when she heard these words about her beloved father, stopped being angry.

Rashi the Teacher

It was almost noon when Rabbi Solomon returned from the vineyards with his two other daughters.

"There is a new student, who has come from Rameru," said his wife. "But before you see him, sit down. Let me wash your hands and serve you your meal."

"From Rameru!" said Rashi with delight. "He must be the son of my old friend Samuel. How many days and nights Samuel and I spent together over the Talmud! Where is the boy?"

The wife sighed but said nothing. The food would have to wait. Now the idea of helping another student understand the Torah made Rashi forget everything else.

Meir came out of the room where he had been resting, and greeted the master of the house with respect. "My father and mother are in good health, and send greetings," young Meir said to his new teacher. "I feel as though I have always known you, Rabbi. All my life my father has been teaching me Talmud with your explanations."

"They are not my explanations," said Rashi. "I learned them from the writings of the rabbis, and from my honored teachers at Worms and in the academies of the Rhineland. Only now and then do I add my own ideas. Sometimes I feel I have to translate a word into French. Mostly I have put the old commentaries into simple language, sentence by sentence, so a young student can understand as he reads."

"My father told me you were modest about your work," said Meir. "He also told me that you were born on the day the last Gaon of Babylonia died, so that glory should not depart out of Israel."

Jochebed ran forward. "Don't you see you are embarrassing my father? He hates to be praised. Look—" and she handed Meir some parchment pages—"here is the work he did yesterday. This is what you can study with him."

Rashi smiled and placed his hand on his daughter's head. "She feels that this work is partly hers, and she is right. That is why she wants you to see it."

"Did she really help you with it?" asked Meir.

"Of course," said Rashi. "This is a commentary on the Bible. I try to explain each sentence, answering the questions a student might ask. My daughters are my constant students, and the questions that they ask help me know what explanations are needed."

"Tell him about the question I asked yesterday," said Jochebed. "I asked how the Torah could say that 'God finished on the seventh day, His work which He had made.' How could it say that God finished on the Sabbath? That seems to say He worked on the Sabbath."

"And a very good question it was, too," said Rashi. "You may read here the answers I have found."

Meir took the closely-written page and read the careful Hebrew handwriting:

Rabbi Simeon says: A human being who does not know the time and the moment exactly, needs to add time from the weekday to the Holyday (begin the Sabbath early, so there is no mistake). But the Holy One, who knows time and moments exactly, entered the Sabbath at the exact instant that ended the sixth day, so it seemed as if He had finished His work on the Sabbath. Another explanation: What was still lacking in the world at the end of the sixth day? Rest. There came the Sabbath, there came rest; thus was ended and completed the work of creation.

"I like the second one better," said Jochebed.

The Rashi Chapel in the city of Worms, supposed to have been the synagogue where the great commentator worshiped.

"I have another question on the same subject," said Meir. "I have always wondered how the Torah can tell us that God rested at all. God is all-powerful. Why should He need rest?"

"It is to teach us," said Rashi, "that if God allows the Torah to say that He rested, how much more should poor tired man know that he should rest on the Sabbath."

"Now that is sensible," said Meir to Jochebed.

"There is an interesting sentence I worked on this morning, before dawn," said Rashi. "It is this: 'Noah was a righteous man in his generation.'"

"What is the problem in that sentence?" asked Meir.

"I have found some writers who say that Noah should be given extra credit for being a good man, because he lived among wicked people, the generation of the flood. They say that if he had lived at a time when people were good, he would have been even more righteous.

"Then there are some who say he was not so good after all: only in comparison with his own generation was he considered righteous, but if he had lived at the time of Abraham he would not have been considered so."

"I like the first one better," said Jochebed.

"I will be working soon on the story of Abraham," said Rashi. "My children have asked me about the order God gave to Abraham to sacrifice his son Isaac. They are unhappy to think that God could have wanted such a thing. I will have to explain that He never intended the sacrifice to take place. He never said, 'Sacrifice thy son,' but 'Take thy son.' He was testing Abraham, but from the beginning he planned to spare Isaac."

"This commentary will help every student from now on, not only your little girls," said Meir.

And while the dinner still waited, Rashi and Meir sat down to study further the words of the Torah.

The Family of Rashi

Meir was not the only student who came to the house of Rashi; Many young scholars be-

Inside view of the Rashi Chapel.

came part of his household. After they had studied with the master for some years, they could go back to their towns and become teachers themselves.

Some of the young students became even more a part of Rashi's family than those who stayed a few years.

It was not many years after he first came to Rashi's house that Meir ben Samuel married Jochebed, the girl who had met him at the door with a broom.

You can be sure that Meir thought his bride was the loveliest and the brightest of Rashi's three learned daughters. You can be sure, too, about the scholars who married Jochebed's two sisters, that each thought the same about his own wife.

But it may be that Jochebed could be considered the best. That is because she had the most wonderful children. She became the mother of three little boys, who grew up to become famous teachers and commentators themselves. They were named Samuel, Isaac and Jacob. Samuel became so well-known that, like his grandfather, he was given a special name made up of his initials: Rashbam, from Rabbi Shmuel ben Meir. Jacob was widely known and beloved under the name of Rabbenu Tam. He was a prince, a leader and an adviser to his people.

The grandsons devoted themselves to deep study of the Talmud. They wrote their own commentaries, but they did not want them to take the place of the great writings of Rashi, their honored grandfather. They said, "We are merely adding some comments to his work." The Hebrew word for "additions" is Tosafot, and the commentators that followed Rashi were called Tosafists.

It happened that the way of explanation of the Rashbam was quite different from the way of his grandfather. Sometimes in his writings the younger man contradicted the older. The grandfather, always gentle and modest, is sup- posed to have said, "I feel that the way of my disciples may be better than my way."

After Rashi Died

The work of Rashi was so important, and the man Rashi was so loved, that after his death people kept talking about him. Everybody had some story to show how great he was and how kind and good.

In the town of Worms there was a narrow alley with walls on both sides. There was a place in one wall that seemed to be hollowed out. The people said that before Rashi was born his mother had been walking in the alley, and was in danger of being run over by a wagon. The wall curved in to make a space for her to get out of the way!

In towns all over the French and German countrysides, all the way to the city of Prague, and even in more distant communities, people would point out a chair Rashi was supposed to have sat in, a street where he might have walked.

Rashi could not in his lifetime have visited all the Jewish communities that longed for the honor of his presence. But in one way he really was present in every town. His commentaries, his helpful works for students of the Bible and the Talmud, were in every Jewish school in the world.

During Rashi's time there was no printing; it had not yet been invented. But 400 years later, in the year 1475, the first Hebrew book to be printed by Jews in all the world was published in Italy. The very first book which the Jews thought worthy of being printed was the commentary of Rashi on the Bible.

To this day, whenever a student has a question about the meaning of a word or sentence in the Bible, the first thing he is told is "See what Rashi says."

SELECTIONS FROM RASHI

Commentary on the sentences from the Torah:

"Hear O Israel: The Lord our God, the Lord is One. And thou shalt love the Lord thy God with all thy heart, and with all thy soul, and with all thy might. And these words, which I command thee this day, shall be upon thy heart; and thou shalt teach them diligently to thy children."

"The Lord our God, the Lord is One": *The Lord, who is our God now, is not accepted as God by all nations; but in the future He will truly be the one Lord of the earth, as it is said, "For I will change the nations that they may call upon the name of the Lord," and "In that day the Lord will be One, and His name One."*

*   *   *

"And thou shalt love": *Perform his commandments out of love. One cannot compare him who acts out of love to him who acts from fear, who serves his master out of fear; for when the feared master becomes too oppressive, the servant runs away from him.*

*   *   *

"With all thy heart": *With all your desires. Another interpretation is, that your heart should not be divided but whole in its devotion to the Lord.*

*   *   *

"And with all thy might": *This means with all your possessions. There are men whose wealth is more beloved by them than themselves. Another interpretation is: With whatever God gives to you, whether good or bad; even in sorrow, serve Him.*

*   *   *

"And these words which I command thee this day": *Let these words not be like an old law which nobody obeys any more, but like a new one, just given, which everyone runs to meet.*

*   *   *

"Unto thy children": *These are pupils. We find everywhere that pupils are called children, as it is said, "You are the children of the Lord." So is the teacher called "father" by his pupils.*

Judah Ha-Levi

1075 - 1141

"Once upon a time, in a far-off land, there was a mighty king. He was good and wise; but he was not happy. One night he had a dream . . ."

Would you like to hear the rest of this story? It sounds like the beginning of a legend of the Arabian nights. In reality it is nothing of the sort, but the telling of a true fact of history, and the introduction to a very serious book of Jewish philosophy.

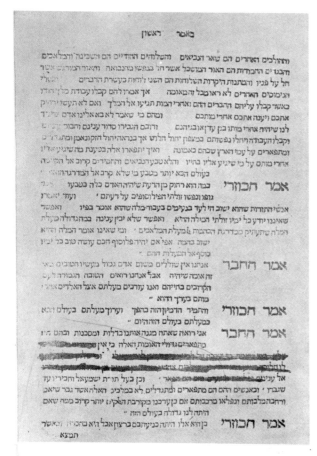

A page from the first edition of the Kuzari. You can see the dialogue form of the writing. To the side of the page stand the words: "Said the Kuzari," and "Said the Haver (meaning rabbi)," introducing their statements.

Judah Ha-Levi wrote this book, the *Kuzari*, in such an interesting way, and with such good logic and fine thoughts, that its readers enjoyed it more than any tale of the Arabian nights. For Judah, though he was a doctor, a scholar and a scientist in his time, was first of all a writer.

Home of Samuel Ha-Levi in Toledo, Spain.

When he was still a boy in the city of Toledo in Spain, Judah Ha-Levi was known for his writing. We can picture how one of his older friends might have come to him for help.

"You are so good with your pen, Judah," said Simon, a lad in his teens. "I wonder if you can do me a favor."

"I'll be glad to help you if I can," answered Judah.

"This is most important," said Simon, "and must be kept secret. Do you know Esther, the daughter of Solomon?"

"Yes, I know her," said Judah, who now understood.

Simon's face grew red. "I think she's the most beautiful girl in the world, but I can't tell her. What I want to do is to send her a poem telling her how I feel."

Judah smiled. "And you want me to write the poem? It's not as easy and as quick as you think. But I can show you some poems I already have. You can choose the one you like."

Simon looked through the pile of papers in amazement. "Where did you find time to write all these?" he asked. Some were in Arabic, some in Hebrew; some were rhymed like the popular songs of Spain, and some were written in the style of the Hebrew Psalms.

Judah shrugged. "I just do them for practice, when my eyes need a rest from studying," he said.

Simon soon found a good poem for his purpose. It began this way:

Amid the groves of Paradise you stand,
  In beauty like a flowering myrtle tree;
And like Orion and his starry band,
  You grace the heavens in your brilliancy.

"Her name means 'star' and also 'myrtle,'" Simon was pleased to point out. "She'll think the poem was written just for her."

Although Judah never boasted, everyone in Toledo soon seemed to know of the wonderful talent of the young poet.

Physician and Scholar

When Judah was a little older, his father made a decision, one made by many Jewish parents throughout the ages.

"Judah is my only child," said Samuel Ha-Levi. "I must see that his mind and soul are nourished as they should be.

"Here in Toledo he has been able to learn

Arms or insignia of the Ha-Levi family.

Rabbi Isaac Alfasi, great teacher of the 11th century.

the science of the Moslems and Christians. He has studied the philosophy of Aristotle the Greek, who was a very wise man but a heathen. Aristotle believed that God created the world; but he never understood that the same God who set the universe on its course wants men to be good and kind to each other.

"This great lesson can be learned only through religion. I want my son to learn his Jewish tradition so that he may be a good Jew as well as a learned man."

For his advanced Jewish education, Judah's parents had to send their son away from home, to study in the city of Lucena at the school of the revered teacher Isaac Alfassi.

There may have been tears when young Judah left his home. Later there were tears of joy rather than sorrow, when the parents heard reports on the great progress their son was making in his studies and in his writing. Every report told how their gentle son was loved by all who knew him.

Eventually Judah came back to Toledo to practice as a physician. Though he was one of the most famous doctors of his day, he felt that he was only a humble assistant to God, the true Healer. He wrote:

My medicines are of Thee, and bespeak
Thy art—whether good or evil, strong or weak.
The choice is in Thy hands, never in mine:
Knowledge of all things fair and foul is Thine.
I heal not with some power fixed in me,
But only through the healing sent from Thee.

He continued to write, although it was hard to find time in his busy life. He wrote hundreds of poems of prayer and thanksgiving, many still to be found in prayerbooks.

When Judah Ha-Levi married, the light of his life was his one daughter, who became as learned as Rashi's daughters. Later there was a grandson, named Judah also, in honor of his famous grandfather.

The Kuzari

Judah Ha-Levi's life was one of love. His love for his fellowman he showed through his practice of medicine. His love for learning was shown in a lifetime of study; his love for the Torah, in a life of piety and observance of the commandments.

His love for his people he showed in his greatest work, called *Al Khazari* in Arabic, the language it was written in, and *Ha-Kuzari* in its Hebrew translation.

The king in the book was Bulan, ruler of the Khazars, a heathen tribe which had lived long before, in a province of southern Russia. The book tells of this king and of imaginary conversations he had with a rabbi.

This is how it begins:

Once upon a time there was a king. He ruled over the great tribe of the Khazars. He was a good and wise king, and tried to do his best for his people. He prayed and offered sacrifices to the gods of his country. Yet he was not happy.

One night he dreamed a dream. It appeared as if an angel spoke to him, saying, "Your way of thinking is pleasing to God, but not your way of acting."

The king awoke with the resolve to please

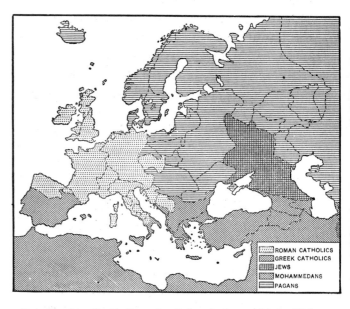

Map showing distribution of religions in Europe in the 10th century. The Jewish population includes the kingdom of the Khazars, which this mapmaker thought was very large.

God. He devoted himself to the service of his temple and of the Khazar religion.

But again the angel came at night and repeated, "Your desire is pleasing to God, but not your actions."

The king awoke perplexed. "Who can tell me the way a man should live?" he asked.

He sent for a philosopher, who spent his days thinking about the universe.

"I cannot tell you how to please God," said the philosopher. "In my philosophy, God is not interested and cannot possibly care what people do. He is perfect in Himself and does not concern Himself with anything else."

The king was not satisfied. "I must find a religion that seems true to me, that tells me how to live in the way that God desires," he said.

Now the three religions of one God were Islam, the religion of the Moslems, followers of Mohammed; Christianity, the religion of many nations of Europe; and Judaism, the religion of a small people scattered throughout the world.

The king said, "Bring to me a Christian teacher and a learned man of the Moslems"; but he did not send for a Jew, because he thought, "They are a small people, of no influence."

The Christian told the king of his faith. "I believe," he said, "that God lives forever, and that He created the world and mankind; that God loves the world; that He has made His will known to man through His prophets, and that He desires man to love his neighbor. In short, I believe all that is written in the Torah and the records of the children of Israel."

He then went on to tell the doctrine of the Christians, and ended by saying, "Yet our whole faith is based on the truth of the divine law of Moses."

The king then turned to the Moslem scholar, who told him, "I believe that God is one, eternal, and without form or body." He went on with the message of Mohammed about this world and life after death, as told in the holy book, the Koran.

"How do we know that God really tells us hese things?" the king asked.

"You can see that the Koran is true." said the Moslem, "because it begins with the Torah of Moses, which everyone knows is true."

"The books of the New Testament are a continuation of the Bible of the Jews," said the Christian.

"I see," said the king, "that both of your religions depend on the Jewish Bible, and both of you agree that the beliefs of the Jews are true."

"That is so," said the Christian and the Moslem.

"Then I must send for a Jewish teacher," said the king of the Khazars.

It is easy to guess what happened. The king and his whole kingdom became converts to Judaism, and the king spent the rest of his life studying his faith and trying to be a good Jew.

The kingdom of the Khazars had disappeared long before Judah Ha-Levi wrote about them. The Khazar people had mixed with other Jews of Europe and Asia. But the story of the good king and the wise rabbi who taught him about the Jewish religion remains in this work by Judah Ha-Levi.

The Lesson of the Story

Why did Judah Ha-Levi write this book?

The Jews in Spain were few in number, and surrounded by men of other faiths. Often wise men of different religions would argue about what was the best way to live. Often Jews did not know how to answer these arguments, or how to explain their own beloved religion.

Sometimes the Jews of Spain, living under the rule of Christians or Moslems, felt that their own people was small and unimportant.

Judah Ha-Levi loved his people and wanted them to have pride in their faith, and hope for their future. The *Kuzari* made the Jews proud of their religion.

In the book, the rabbi answers questions asked by the king, and thus explains Judaism for the readers of the book. The king, for example, asks, "Are not the many prayers and blessings that a Jew must say a heavy burden for him?"

The rabbi answers that the saying of blessings, of thanking God, makes the Jew a happy man. When a man thanks God for opening his eyes in the morning, for giving him freedom, and the strength to do his work, he can face the day with joy instead of complaint. When he thanks God for food, he reminds himself of how fortunate he is, to have enough of everything. Noticing and being thankful for good things will make a man appreciate his life, and be happy.

The rabbi tells the king that the Jewish people can be called the heart of the world. Like the heart in the body, it feels and understands the most. Like the heart also, the Jewish people suffers when there is trouble anywhere.

This was to comfort the Jews for their sorrows. Even suffering showed their important place in the world.

Love for the Land of Israel

The last lesson of the *Kuzari* is a message of love for Palestine, the holy land of Israel. Judah Ha-Levi wrote: "Jerusalem can only be rebuilt when Israel yearns for it so much that they embrace her stones and dust."

In his youth he had written poems of love for Zion:

> My heart is in the east;
>   I languish in the west:
> How then can fun or feast
>   Find favor in my breast?
> My vows again arise,
>   But hope to fill them wanes
> While Zion fettered lies,
>   And I in Arab chains.
>
> Fain would I flee from Spain
>   And seek a fairer strand,
> My dear delight to gain
>   In Israel's Holy Land.

When Judah Ha-Levi was old, full of years and honor, his lifelong yearning would not let him rest. He left the city of Cordova, the center of learning and of Jewish life in Spain, where his daughter and grandson lived, and started on his last journey.

During the stormy voyage across the Mediterranean Sea, when it seemed that the small sailing ship might go down, the aged poet was strengthened by his love of Zion. He had written:

> Oh city filled with beauty, by God and mankind blest,
> For thee my soul is longing from the limits of the west.
>
> Oh that I might on eagles' wings fly free of ocean's fears
> To thee, so that thy sacred dust might mingle with my tears.

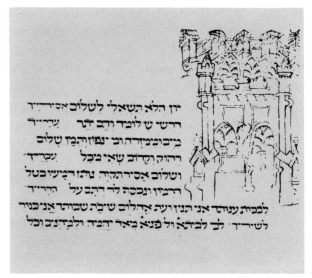

Opening lines of the "Ode to Zion" by Judah Ha-Levi. From a 15th century manuscript.

When Judah landed in Alexandria in Egypt, the Jews of that city greeted him with delight and honor. They persuaded him to stay and recover from his journey.

"Egypt is favored by God's presence too," said his host. "In Egypt God showed many miracles and favors to Israel, and inspired the greatest prophet, Moses."

"All that God did for the children of Israel was done either in the land of Israel or for the sake of the land of Israel," said Judah.

"To journey to Jerusalem would be dangerous," said another. "The Temple is destroyed; only a part of one wall remains. The country is ruled by strangers, and Jews are not safe."

"If I had just time to kiss the earth of Zion, and then die, I would die happy," Judah would reply.

Because of this well-known desire of Judah Ha-Levi, a moving legend grew up among his people. The story tells that, old and feeble, and disregarding the advice of his friends, he left Egypt and continued the dangerous journey to the shores of the Holy Land and the very city of Jerusalem.

There, as he knelt in tears to kiss the holy earth where the Temple once stood, an Arab horseman struck him down with his spear.

The manner of death, however, is not nearly so important as the manner of life. The life of Judah Ha-Levi was one of love and loyalty, a life in which all his talents were devoted to serving his people, and bringing joy and understanding to their hearts.

SELECTIONS FROM JUDAH HA-LEVI

O Lord, where shall I find Thee?
All hidden and exalted is Thy place.
And where shall I not find Thee?
Full of Thy glory is the infinite space.

I have sought Thy nearness;
With all my heart have I called Thee;
And going out to meet Thee
I found Thee coming toward me.

* * *

According to the Jewish point of view, the one who serves God best is not one who separates himself from the world, or hates life, which has been given to him by God. On the contrary, he loves the world and a long life, because it gives him opportunities of doing good and of deserving the World to Come.

* * *

A king is not necessary for the government of a people. It is possible that a people should have many leaders, working together to give judgment in all matters. Why should their term of office not be for one year, or for three years, like the term of a hired servant? When other judges and officers take over, they will correct any wrong that the first ones have committed. Why should their power not be regulated according to law? It is common sense that the majority should have the right to decide on a law. A one-man ruler is much more likely to do wrong, through foolishness or anger, than a group ruling together. If one of them wants to do wrong, the others will stop him. Since they know they will not be in office forever, and can be brought to account for what they do, they will be more careful.

* * *

I think that kings were first set up to rule not by the people's choice, but by force. The one that was strongest took over. Even these were expected to serve the people, but they made themselves masters, and they leave their land to their children for ever. This has been a curse to the world.

Maimonides

1135 - 1204

A thirteen-year-old boy rolled over in his sleep, and suddenly sat up. His bedroom, and indeed the whole world, seemed dark and silent. In the bed next to his, his small brother David breathed peacefully.

Then there came the sound of distant shouting.

Wide awake, Moses left his bed and moved to the arched window, where open hangings let in an autumn breeze and the faint light of a half moon. He looked out at the stone houses and the well-planted gardens of his familiar street. Through the trees he could see a glimmer of the Guadalquivir River.

Moses turned his head. Far off, somewhere near the Jews' Gate where many of his friends lived, there was a red glow in the sky. At that moment, the boy heard sounds of voices and running feet in his own home.

Eldad, the family's chief servant, entered the room, holding a small oil-lamp.

"Moses, Moses!" he said in a low voice that was full of distress. "Wake up David and get dressed. They're here; they've captured the city."

"The Almohades?" asked Moses.

"Yes, they've come, the wild ones, who will kill everyone who is not a Moslem. The Koran or the sword!"

"We will be ready," said Moses. Eldad left to help the rest of the household.

West wall of 11th century synagogue of Cordova.

Jews' Gate in Cordova, leading to the Jewish quarter.

"In my own city, Cordova," thought Moses sadly as he quickly dressed. "We were prepared for this but never believed it. Who would think this could happen in a civilized city, where Jews and Christians and Moslems have lived in peace together for years?"

He touched his brother's shoulder gently. "David," he said.

The six-year-old woke slowly. "I don't want to get up," he murmured.

"You must," said Moses. "Wash your hands and get dressed. Put on warm clothing and your heaviest shoes, and take your cloak."

David admired and always obeyed his older brother. He jumped from his bed. As he started to dress he asked, "How can we pray now? It's too early for *Shaharit*. It's still dark outside."

"We will pray later," said Moses. "Now we're going on a trip. All of us, Mother and Father too."

"Can I take my ball?" David asked.

The Loss of the Books

Moses stood still for a moment, his heart filling with pain. The thought of all he must leave behind struck him. The books, the shelves of beautiful, bulky, hand-written manuscripts—the *Tanach*, the eighteen volumes of the Talmud, commentaries of the rabbis, writings in Arabic on astronomy, medicine,

Calle de Maimonides, Cordova.

mathematics, the philosophy of Aristotle—all the books his father Maimon had gathered, and that he, Moses, had grown up with, studied and loved, would have to be left.

In the small cart which they would be able to take with them, the family had planned to take only what was absolutely necessary for travel, plus hidden jewels that might be exchanged for money wherever they wandered.

Moses took his brother's small hand. "You may take your toy," he said. David ran to the corner of the room and picked up the large ball his mother had made for him of strips of cloth. The two boys hurried down to the courtyard of the house.

There were waiting the boys' father, the fine, dignified scholar who was the *dayan*, the head of the Jewish community of Cordova; their mother Sara; and three Moslem servants, who wanted to go with the family.

The mother ran to her two sons. She had been crying, but now her face was calm.

"Here is some food for each of you," she said. "We will eat on the road, as soon as we're far enough from the city."

"Is everything packed, Mother?" asked Moses.

"Everything we can take," said the mother sadly.

The father, Maimon, went to the gate and returned.

"I'm afraid they have set fire to the large synagogue," he said.

Moses looked at his own house. "Then our home too, and our books, may also go up in smoke?"

David tugged at his big brother's arm. "Don't worry about the books, Moses. You've read them all already."

Moses and his father did not smile. As they turned to leave the home where both of them had been born, Moses said slowly, "Yes, only what is in my head is safe. Education is never lost. No matter what happens, no matter where we have to go, I will use it in God's service."

The sound of shouting grew nearer. The small sad group left the city.

The Wandering Family

The family of Maimon was only one of the families that were made refugees by the fierce Almohades. In town after town, where the Jews had lived well for generations, they found themselves forced to flee from the choice that was offered to them: "The Koran or the sword." The Golden Age the Jews had enjoyed in Spain seemed at an end.

Maimon's family first went to another Spanish city, Port Almeria; but the Almohades soon reached there. There were years of danger, of traveling from one place to another.

Wherever they went, the Jewish community would make them welcome. Even secret Jews, who pretended that they were Moslems in order to live in peace, would try to meet Maimon and talk over their problems with him and his son Moses.

Father and sons continued to study together through all their travels. Little David, as he grew up, became the practical business man of the family. More and more he took care of trade and money matters, allowing his father and brother to devote their time to Torah.

Finally the family left Spain, going on the long sea-voyage across the Mediterranean to the city of Fez in North Africa.

If the family had hoped to find it easier to live in Fez than in Spain, they were sadly disappointed. The Moslems in North Africa were like the Almohades, and would not allow anyone to live there unless he admitted that Mohammed was the prophet of God.

A Letter to the Secret Jews

The Jews were forced to pretend that they believed in the religion of Mohammed. Secretly they kept all Jewish laws that they could, and taught their children Torah. Some who were discovered were put to death.

"All we can hope," was the common saying, "is that the Messiah will come and save us."

A rabbi of the time, living in a safer country, wrote a letter against the secret Jews. "If they say they are Moslems," he wrote, "they are no longer Jews, and can never become Jews again. They should be willing to give up their lives before becoming Moslems."

Maimon had a midnight meeting of some of the secret Jews at his home.

"Should we refuse to obey the government, tell them we will never become Moslems, and be put to death?" asked one man. "Should we let our little children be killed too?"

"No!" shouted other voices. "God can't want us all to die."

A young man stood up. "I know what I will do," he said. "According to Jewish law we are already lost. We have said that we believe in Mohammed and his teaching, the Koran, in order to save our lives. We can never be forgiven; we can never be Jews

again. Let us give up trying to be Jews at all, and really become Moslems."

Others stood up, shouting. Some cried, "No, no!"

It would be dangerous if anyone knew the Jews were having a meeting. Maimon tried in vain to quiet the group. The meeting finally broke up in confusion; and the secret Jews went down different roads to their homes.

Moses, the son of Maimon, had used his learning often before to give help and advice to his fellow Jews. Now he said to his father: "I will not sleep until I have found a message of hope for the Jews of the Moslem countries."

All night Moses worked on a letter to the

A holograph, meaning a page written in the original handwriting of the author, of Maimonides. This is a page of the *Guide to the Perplexed*, written in Arabic in Hebrew letters, by the Rambam himself.

Jews. He found sentences in Bible and Talmud that showed how important it is to save life, and how sinners who repent are still members of their people.

He said that it was praiseworthy to die rather than to give up Judaism, even in words; but that not every Jew should be expected to die as a martyr, *al kiddush hashem*. To save their lives through saying that Mohammed was a true prophet, and then to keep as much of the Torah as possible, was the course open to the Jews.

When the letter was completed, it was sent secretly, from hand to hand, to the Jews of Fez. Copies were smuggled out to other Jewish communities. For the first time, Jews living under the danger and difficulty of Moslem rule had some comfort and hope.

Finding a Resting-place

The final words of the letter of young Maimonides were a message to himself and his family. "All Jews who possibly can," he wrote, "must leave the countries where such conditions exist. They must go to a place where they can be full Jews once more."

The father followed the advice of his son. Again there was a long and dangerous journey, this time to the holy land of Palestine.

Heartbreak waited for the family of Maimon and for any Jews who visited the homeland. The Jews of Palestine lived in poverty, with no hope except for the coming of the Messiah. Arabs had overrun the land, destroying trees and farmland. The invasion of the first Crusade had further devastated the coun-

Remains of a Crusader wall in the city of Acre.

try; and the Christian armies claimed the holy cities as their own.

In a short time, the family moved on to Egypt. There, in the city of Fostat, near Cairo, they at last found some rest.

The Moslem ruler, the Sultan Saladin, was an intelligent and understanding man. Under his rule there was peace. There were not so many schools and libraries in Fostat as there had been in Cordova, but learning was respected.

Moses Maimonides became a well-known citizen. He was a scholar in philosophy, astronomy and medicine. His greatest interest was in his studies and in the writing of books he had been planning for many years, through all his travels.

David carried on a trade in jewels. He traveled to far-off countries buying and selling his precious stones. Traders lent him money so that he could buy his wares, and on his return he was able to pay them back more than they had given.

Then misfortune struck. Sea-travel was filled with danger in those days. David's ship was lost in a storm, and David never returned.

The Jews of India, separated for hundreds of years from other Jews of the world, have a legend that David Maimonides was shipwrecked on their shore, taught them Torah

Some Jews of India.

which they had forgotten and then died in India.

Moses Maimonides never recovered from the loss of his only, beloved brother. Besides his grief, he now had other problems. Money had to be paid back to David's business partners. From then on, Maimonides had to work hard as a physician to support himself and pay his debts. He was named Rabbi of his city, but, although this added to his hours of work, he would take no payment.

The Commentary on the Mishnah

Yet he continued to write. His Commentary on the Mishnah was the first one that explained the laws of the Mishnah clearly and simply. His mind was much keener than that of the ordinary man, but he had the gift of explaining things so that all who read could understand.

In this commentary, Maimonides included his Thirteen Principles of Faith, which are said every day in the Morning Service. Among the principles that he said a Jew must believe are these: that God is One; that God lives forever; that He is not a body, that He is never in human form; that God made His will known to men through the prophets, and that the greatest of all prophets was Moses.

Maimonides was soon known all over the world. The Jews called him the Rambam, according to the first letters of his Hebrew name, Rabbi Moshe ben Maimon.

The non-Jews also knew of his brilliant mind and great learning. The Sultan Saladin himself asked Maimonides to be his court physician. From then on, the scholar was busier than ever.

An Arab wrote that King Richard the Lion-Hearted, when he came to that part of the world on a Crusade, tried to get the famous sage to follow him back to England and be his doctor. Maimonides was too loyal to the Sultan and to his Jewish community, to leave and go to the distant land of England.

With all his many duties, as doctor, rabbi and adviser, Maimonides kept writing. He wrote many articles on health and medicine.

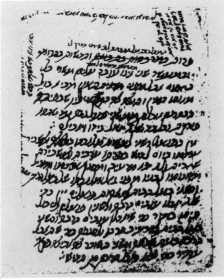

A page written by Maimonides.

He wrote a letter of hope to the Jews of Yemen, who thought that God had forgotten them and that they should give up being Jews. "God is testing you," he wrote, "but God has not forgotten you."

The Mishneh Torah

Ten years after the Commentary on the Mishnah, Maimonides had completed his great work called the *Mishneh Torah*, or Second Torah. He wrote this in Hebrew, although all his other works were in Arabic. He wanted it to be used by students who had knowledge of Hebrew and the laws of Israel, but who were not experts in the law.

The Mishneh Torah listed all the laws for daily life and for religious observances that can be found in the Talmud. The Talmud is not arranged in a definite order, because it was written over a long period of time, with the discussions of many scholars included. Maimonides arranged the laws in fourteen sections, so anyone could look them up. Such an arrangement is called a Code.

Since he was a doctor, the Rambam included much good advice about eating, exercise, and other daily concerns. He said that it was a *mitzvah*, a religious duty, to keep oneself healthy.

Guide for the Perplexed

Nobody knew more about the problems of the Jews than Maimonides. He saw how troubled they were, living often among unfriendly neighbors, sometimes forced to hide their religion.

The Moslems were more learned at that time than any other group. They translated the wisdom of the world into their language, Arabic. They studied the philosophy of Aristotle and made it their own.

After ten years of work, Maimonides produced his most important book, the *Guide for the Perplexed*. It was a book of philosophy which showed how the beliefs of Judaism and the beliefs of Aristotle could go together. Both Aristotle and the Torah said that God is One and that man's purpose in life is to make himself pure and perfect.

Maimonides was a doctor and a man of science. To his study of Jewish tradition he brought the same clear thinking he applied to the study of a medical book. Whatever seemed unscientific in the Bible he was able to explain as not being necessary for a Jew to believe.

There were some who found it hard to believe in the miracles in the Bible. They did not want their Judaism to depend on believing that, for instance, the sun stood still for Joshua. The Rambam said that the miracles could be explained; but that, in any case, miracles were not needed to prove the truth of the Bible. They could be left out and the great lessons of the Bible would still stand by themselves.

Some Jews were embarrassed by the fact that animal sacrifices had been offered in the Temple. Moslems said that they were like offerings to a pagan god, who was supposed to eat what his worshipers brought him.

Maimonides explained that the sacrifices were not offered as a favor to God. What God wanted was the righteousness, repent-

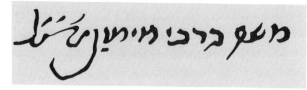

He was often ill, and always tired and over-worked.

One day he was pleased to receive a letter from Samuel ibn Tibbon, a scholar and translator who lived in France. He told that he was busy translating the *Guide* into Hebrew, so that all Jews, not only those in Arabic-speaking countries, could read it. Ibn Tibbon wrote also that his greatest desire was to travel to Egypt and meet the Rambam face to face.

Maimonides answered that he was over-joyed that a great scholar was translating his book. He himself would not have had time. But, the Rambam wrote, it would not be worthwhile for Ibn Tibbon to take the long journey. There would be no time for the two men to talk to each other.

"My duties to the Sultan are very heavy," wrote Maimonides. "I am obliged to visit him every morning, and when he or any of his children, or his wives, are ill, I may not leave Cairo, but must stay almost the whole day in the palace. . . . Even if nothing unusual happens, I do not return home till the after-noon. Then I am almost dying with hunger. I find the front room filled with people, both Jews and Gentiles, friends and foes, a mixed multitude, all waiting for me."

The letter goes on to tell how there was hardly any time to eat even his one meal of the day, because of the many patients and the many persons wanting advice. Even on the Sabbath he was busy, considering the prob-lems of the Jewish community.

Maimonides became known to Moslems and Christians, as well as Jews, as the greatest thinker and the most skillful healer of his day.

A page from the first printed edition of Maimonides' "Guide," now in the library of the Jewish Theological Seminary.

ance, and exalted feelings of the people, that were necessary for the sacrifices. The people thought at that time that the bringing of sacrifices was the right way to worship; but the true service was in the prayers and thoughts of the worshipers.

Years of Hard Work

Maimonides, greatest physician of his time, could not always keep himself in good health.

The Moslems called him Abu-Amram. An Arab poet wrote of him as a doctor, comparing him to Galen, the greatest physician of ancient times:

Galen's art heals only the body,
  But Abu-Amram's the body and soul.
With his wisdom he could heal the sickness of
  ignorance.

There were those who thought that Maimonides had too much power, and had taken too much upon himself. Some said his *Mishneh Torah* discouraged students from reading the original Talmud; some felt he put forward his own ideas rather than the true ideas of the Torah. They felt that students should go back only to the great original sources, and not learn things in a simple or codified form from a modern teacher.

But for most of his people, during his lifetime and until the present day, Maimonides was the greatest mind of the Middle Ages and the greatest teacher as well. Of him we say:

From Moses until Moses, there arose no one like Moses.

SELECTIONS FROM MOSES MAIMONIDES

A young boy is brought to a teacher. The object of teaching the boy is, of course, to enable him to gain knowledge and to reach the highest good. But the boy is too young to appreciate the advantages of knowledge. The teacher will encourage the pupil to study by offering him things that are attractive to a child. He will say, "Read, and I will give you good things to eat." The little one reads, not because he finds pleasure in the book or knows that he will be the better for reading it, but because of the sweets that have been promised to him.

When he becomes a little older the things he used to desire will seem unimportant. He must be offered greater reward. The teacher will say, "Read, and you shall have new shoes and fine clothes." Later the prize is again raised, and he is promised money. At last, when he is grown up, the teacher says, "Study much, and you may become a president or a judge, and people will give you great honor." And the young man learns, hoping for honor and glory.

All of this is unworthy, but it is necessary because the human spirit is narrow and looks for rewards.

The object of knowledge is knowledge itself, and living by the law that is learned. There is the saying, "Do not be like servants who serve their master for the sake of reward, but rather be like those who serve without expecting a reward."

A man may study and do good with the hope of reward until he understands the true worth of study and serves purely out of love. Our sages say: "A man should by all means learn Torah and do good deeds, even if it is only with the idea of being rewarded; for eventually he will arrive at the stage of doing the right thing for its own sake."

*   *   *

The soul, like the body, can be healthy or sick. It is healthy when it wants to do what is good; it is ill when it wants to do what is wrong. Those who are ill in spirit imagine that the evil which they desire is good.

When people realize they are sick, they consult a doctor who tells them what they must do, and he prescribes medicines which often are bitter. So too, those who are spiritually ill should consult the sages, who will advise them not to do the evil which seems good to them. Eventually they will be healed.

*   *   *

There are eight degrees of charity, going from the lowest level to the highest:

1. He who gives unwillingly.

2. He who gives cheerfully, but not enough.

3. *He who gives enough, but not till he is asked.*

4. *He who gives before being asked, but directly to the poor man.*

5. *The poor man knows from whom he takes, but the giver does not know who is receiving.*

6. *The giver knows to whom he gives, but the receiver does not know the giver.*

7. *The giver does not know to whom he gives, nor does the poor man know from whom he receives.*

8. *The highest form of charity is to strengthen the hand of the poor by giving him a loan, or joining him in partnership, or training him out of his poverty, to help him establish himself.*

* * *

The reason for our belief in Moses and all other prophets is the fact that they told us to do what was right, and not because they did miracles. If a man told us what we knew was wrong, and against the law, we would not believe him if he also produced miracles.

* * *

God is just and merciful. He gave man the ability to do what He commanded him to; and to keep from doing what He told him not to do. Man does not do anything unless he chooses to do it. This is the principle of Free Will.

* * *

Men may be placed in ten classes: (1) the pious; (2) the impious; (3) the obedient; (4) the disobedient; (5) the blameless; (6) the negligent; (7) the offender; (8) the rebellious; (9) the unbeliever; (10) the penitent. The one who is truly penitent must do four things: give up doing the wrong act; feel sorry for doing it; pray for forgiveness; and never repeat the sin again.

* * *

We must not say that God has rejected us. We must patiently endure our sufferings, and wait with faith for the fulfillment of His promise.

UNIT THREE

PRESERVERS OF THE FAITH

The thirteenth century was a time when Europe seemed to be settling down. Cities grew up and trade routes were traveled as far as India and China. The Moslems were driven out of most of the provinces of Spain. All of Europe was coming under the control of Christian rulers and the Christian Church.

This did not lead to peace for the Jews of Europe. The Pope in Rome wanted to unify the Christian world and stamp out all heretics, those who did not follow the teachings of the Church. Pope Innocent III, a powerful statesman, made the kings and nobles of the continent obey him by saying he would excommunicate them, cut them off from the Church. He declared that the Jews should not be given rest or peace. Under his rule it was decreed that Jews had to wear a special badge to set them off from other men.

A medieval artist's idea of a discussion between Christians and Jews, where the Jews, wearing their strange hats, could not find any answers to the Christians' arguments.

A picture of Jewish priests from a bible history written in the 14th century. The artist thought that Jews of the time of the Bible wore badges of the sort the Jews of his time were forced to wear.

HATE AND INJUSTICE

Jews had often suffered from unjust laws and from outbreaks of violence. With the Crusades, however, their condition became worse. Persecution became the lot of the Jews everywhere.

In most countries, Jews were forced to live in certain poor areas, and not allowed in other parts of the cities. Merchants complained that the Jews had too much business. Soon the Jews, who were not allowed to own land and be farmers, or belong to the guilds of skilled workers, found that they could not be merchants either. One of the few ways they were allowed to support themselves was by lending money and taking it back with interest.

False charges were made against them. They were accused of doing all kinds of wicked deeds against Christians. The Talmud was said to be a book against God. Several times the Talmud was brought to trial in court as though it were a person; witnesses spoke against it, and it was condemned to be destroyed. The burning of Jewish books disgraced many cities of Europe. Tragic as this was, however, it cannot be compared to the slaughter of thousands of innocent people at various times, in every country of Europe, during the late Middle Ages.

The Jews were able to survive because certain rulers protected them. A king was the lord, or owner, of the Jews of his land. They were a group that had to pay him extra heavy taxes; and for this profit he would see to it that nobody else oppressed or stole from them. He might, however, decide he needed more than the Jews could give him, and would expel them from his kingdom and take all their property.

THE JEWS IN ENGLAND

That is what happened in England. A good number of Jews had come to that country from France with William the Conqueror in 1066. The kings protected the Jews, who carried on commerce and money lending, and paid heavy taxes. Nevertheless, there was violence against the Jews at Norwich and at Lincoln, based on false charges of murder. Ignorant or greedy neighbors believed any charge against this despised and separated people.

At the coronation of King Richard the Lionhearted, the mob, inspired by talk of a new crusade, turned on the Jews. Soon after, the Jews of York were besieged in a castle to which they had fled after the townspeople demanded that they convert to Christianity. Following the example of their leader, Rabbi Yom Tov, the Jews killed themselves rather than surrender.

King Henry III was able to "sell" the Jews of the kingdom, as a source of income, to his brother Richard for one year. The kings made sure that they could take most of the profits, through force, holding for ransom, and confiscation.

Finally, in the year 1290, King Edward ordered all Jews to leave England. The debts that were owed to them, and all their property, went to the king.

For almost 400 years, no Jews were allowed

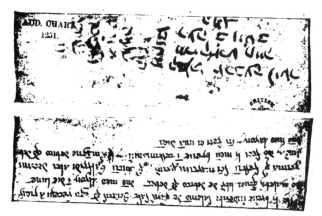

A receipt of Aaron of Lincoln to Richard Maleby, who owed much money to Jews and later led the York massacre.

in England.

FRANCE AND GERMANY

Most of the expelled English Jews went to France. There they did not rest long. A series of expulsions from different provinces of France drove this wandering people from place to place.

Whenever they were expelled, groups of Jews might find a home for a few years in areas controlled by more friendly or tax-hungry noblemen. Many went from one land to another all their lives. A few succeeded in getting to Palestine.

The rulers who so readily expelled the Jews would not let them leave of their own free will. This was illustrated when the saintly Meir of Rothenburg (1220-1293), a Tosafist, head of a large school and leader of the German Jews, tried to lead a group to Palestine. He was arrested and imprisoned by Emperor Rudolph, the first of the Hapsburg rulers of Germany. The emperor did not want the "servants of his treasury" to leave and to take their money with them.

Rabbi Meir refused to allow himself to be ransomed by his people, for he feared it would then become a common practice for rulers to kidnap leading Jews for ransom.

INSIDE THE JEWISH COMMUNITY

In all these troubled times, the Jews found strength in clinging ever more strongly to their religion. Education became even more important than before. The synagogue was the center of each community; morning and evening prayers, study of the Talmud, meetings to discuss needs and problems went on within its walls. The rabbi became the head of the community in all things where the Jews governed themselves.

One thing the Jews did for themselves was take care of the less fortunate ones among them. Taught from their earliest days to help the poor, the widow, the orphan and the stranger, the Jews set an example for the world in their charity and compassion. Refugees from other towns always found a welcome. Jews did not become bitter as a result of their hardships, but rather more generous to the needy and more loyal to each other.

Academies of learning could not produce great original works at such a time. No large schools flourished. Most Jews, however, spent much time in study. Sages exchanged letters and wrote Responsa. Because the Jews were so scattered and because the law was the basis for their lives, codes of law were needed. An important code was that of Rabbi Jacob ben Asher of Spain (1280-1340). It was written in four volumes and was called *Turim,* or "Rows," to remind the readers of the four rows of jewels the high priest used to wear over his heart in the days of the Temple.

The Arabic works of Saadia and Maimonides were translated into Hebrew by Judah and Samuel ibn Tibbon, who lived in Provence, in southern France near Spain. The *Guide to the Perplexed* was widely studied. There were rabbis, however, who felt that the study of philosophy, asking questions and trying to prove the ideas of Judaism, was not a good thing. These rabbis said that Jews

Title-page from the *Arba Turim* by Jacob ben Asher, (Italy, 15th century).

should study only the Talmud, and should devote themselves to obeying the law.

KABBALAH

Besides works on the law, the people also read Midrashim and Hebrew collections of legends and travel stories. Their lives were hard and narrow; they had to look to the pages of books for words of wonder and hope. *Sefer Hasidim,* the "Book of the Pious," written by Judah the Hasid around 1200, was a popular work for generations. Angels and demons and wandering spirits appear in its stories, which show that the good Jew is rewarded and protected by keeping the law.

Trying to rise above the wretched conditions of their life, Jews turned more to the study of *Kabbalah,* that part of tradition which deals with the secrets and mysteries of the universe. Jews, like others, had always tried to figure out exactly how the world was created, how men can understand or come closer to God, what happens to souls after death. Those who devote themselves to such questions are called mystics. The writings of mystics, speaking to the heart and the imagination, were needed by the suffering people.

The chief work of Kabbalah was the *Zohar,* meaning "Brilliance." Moses de Leon (1250-1305) of Spain said that he had found a commentary on the Torah written by Simon bar Yohai in Palestine more than a thousand years before. Simon had been one of the scholars who had taken part in Bar Kochba's rebellion against Rome, and had hidden from the Romans many years. During this time, said Moses de Leon, angels had taught Rabbi Simon the secret meanings of the words of the Torah. The book that de Leon produced was full of strange and wonderful thoughts,

explaining how God had created the world through ten steps, and suggesting how man might purify his soul and rise to a higher level of understanding.

The darker the life of the Jews became, the more they turned to mysticism. In kabbalistic writings, they tried to find answers to questions on why and for how long they were to suffer, and how they might be saved.

TIME OF DISASTER

Every evil that afflicted Europe during the Middle Ages brought woe upon the Jews. Peasants and serfs who lived miserably under the rule of wealthy noblemen could easily be aroused to attack Jews and take their possessions. Nobles who needed more money for war would take it from the Jews. A strong sermon in a village church could bring about a massacre.

Whenever disaster struck, it was natural for people to look for someone to blame. The most terrible plague in history hit Europe in 1349. The Black Death, or bubonic plague, spread so widely in the conditions under which the people lived that a quarter of the population of Europe died.

The world at that time did not know anything about germs, and about rats and insects which help to spread them. In this time of horror, ignorant mobs attacked and killed thousands of Jews, claiming that they must have poisoned the wells to cause the dread disease.

MARRANOS AND THE INQUISITION

Soon afterwards, in Spain, the home of the most respected Jewish community, persecution became even worse than in the rest of Europe. Christian rulers and churchmen, rejoicing that Islam was being driven out of Spain, wished also to see the end of Judaism. Monks aroused the people to riot against the

An amulet supposed to give good luck, with formulas derived from the Zohar and other mystical teachings.

A *Sanbenito*, a victim of the Inquisition who is shown as being sorry for his heresy.

Jews, forcing them to convert or be killed.

Many Jews became "New Christians" in order to save their lives. It soon became known that most of them were not sincere in their new religion. They kept up Jewish customs in secret, hoping for the day when they could become free Jews once more. The name *Marranos,* meaning "pigs," was given to them. This insulting name became a name of honor, for the Marranos were often heroes, keeping loyal to their faith at risk of their lives.

The Church could not stand to see heresy, or any turning away from its teachings. To fight heresy, the Inquisition was established. Officers would seek out those who did not follow every teaching of the Church, bring them to trial, and announce punishment. Prisoners were not allowed to defend themselves, and were tortured to make them confess.

Queen Isabella of Spain was shocked to hear in 1480 that some Marranos were found meeting for a secret *Seder* at Passover. She invited the officers of the Inquisition into her kingdom. Torquemada, head of the Inquisition, became a powerful influence over King Ferdinand and Queen Isabella.

The rulers at first did not want to harm the Jews of Spain, many of whom had been helpful to the court. The learned Jew Isaac Abravanel was chief financial adviser for the kingdom. Torquemada convinced the king and queen that to prevent the New Christians from going back to Judaism, it was necessary to drive out all Jews from Spain.

THE EXPULSION FROM SPAIN

The Expulsion was one of the saddest events in the whole of Jewish history. A quarter of a million Jews were affected. Some were willing to convert. The majority left the country in which their families had lived for hundreds of years. The date of the Expulsion fell, strangely enough, on the ninth day of Av, the day on which the destruction of both Temples is mourned.

On August 2, 1492, the ships carrying the refugees left the harbor—the same day that Christopher Columbus's three ships set out

A procession of officials and victims of the Inquisition in Goa, leading to an Auto-da-Fe.

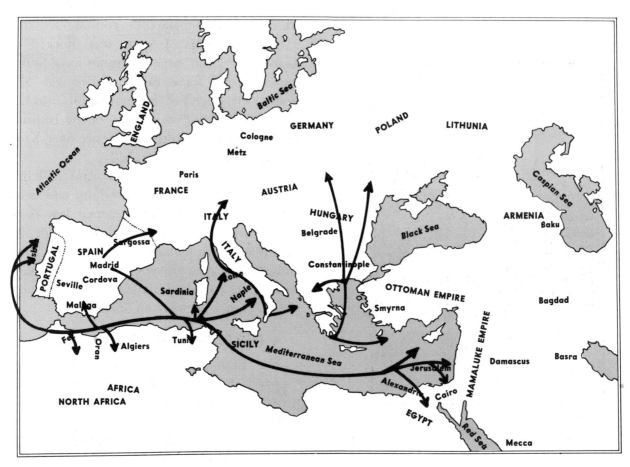

The expulsion from Spain in 1492. The map shows how the first exiles went to Portugal and to Southern Italy; persecution followed and many fled eastward to countries of the Ottoman Empire.

from the same harbor on their voyage to the west.

No one knew of America at that time. It was not yet a place of refuge for exiles. The Jews of Spain fled to nearby Portugal, to North Africa, to the cities of Italy, to Turkey, to any shore that would receive them. Many were killed or sold as slaves, or left stranded to die of illness or starvation. Those who found safety in Portugal were doomed to be followed there by the Inquisition, which converted them all by force.

Isaac Abravanel escaped to Naples, and then later had to flee to Venice. In each place he settled, this brilliant man was an adviser to kings; but the fact that he was a faithful Jew made him a man without a home. Through his difficult and active life, he con-

tinued the writing of a Bible commentary and other works to strengthen Jewish loyalty.

After years of relative safety, the Mendez family, wealthy Spanish-Portuguese Marranos, escaped from Lisbon to Antwerp. The head of the family was a woman, Dona Gracia. In Antwerp, too, they were in danger. When the beautiful daughter Reyna refused to consider any of the noblemen who asked for her hand in marriage, the rumor grew that the family were secret Jews.

Dona Gracia and her family escaped to Venice, and finally to Moslem Turkey, where they were able to be Jews once more. Reyna married her cousin Joseph Nasi. The family set an example of learning, charity, and service. Joseph, appointed a duke by the Sultan, used his wealth to try to settle Jewish refugees in Palestine. War, however, defeated his plan.

THE SCHOOL OF SAFED

Some Spanish-Portuguese Jews and other refugees from Europe did, however, manage to reach Palestine. The city of Safed became a center for mystical studies. There scholars spent their lives in study, prayer, fasting and good deeds. Through goodness they hoped to fight the forces of Satan, the evil angel, who seemed to control so much of the world.

Rabbi Isaac Luria (1534-1572) was an outstanding mystical teacher. He came to Safed from Germany, and was called *Ha-Ashkenazi*, the German, as opposed to the Spanish, or *Sephardi* Jews. From the initials of Ashkenazi Rabbi Isaac, he became known as the *Ari*, which means "lion" in Hebrew.

The Ari believed that souls could be born again and again in different bodies, till they were pure enough to rise into higher form. He thought he was the messenger of the Mes-

The synagogue of the ARI, in Safed, Israel.

siah, who would save the Jews from their exile. His student Hayim Vital helped to spread his teachings. Jews all over the world studied his words, hoping to find in them a way to bring the time of saving nearer.

A scholar of the school of Safed, who had been exiled from Spain as a child, and had lived safely for some time in Turkey, was Joseph Caro (1488-1575). He wished to unite the Jewish people in perfect observance of the law. For this purpose he wrote a commentary on the *Turim,* and then a complete code of laws of daily life for every Jew, called the *Shulhan Arukh,* the "Set Table." He hoped that when the people were one, under one leadership, the Messiah would come.

The hope for a better time, which meant for them hope in the coming of the Messiah, kept the Jews from despair through centuries of persecution. Their devotion to their way of life kept them alive as a people, though it claimed countless martyrs.

The king of Aragon once forced Nachmanides, the greatest Jewish scholar of his day, to enter a public debate on Christianity and Judaism.

"Why do you Jews not accept our Messiah?" the king asked.

"The coming of the Messiah means the coming of a time of peace, brotherhood and justice," said Nachmanides. "As long as the world is still suffering from war, bloodshed and injustice, we cannot believe that the Messiah has already come. We wait for his coming."

Meir of Rothenburg

1220 - 1293

A tired group of travelers, walking on foot through the German countryside, were looking anxiously for a place to spend the night.

Their leader, a fine, dignified old man with a long beard, stopped to look around at the fields that stretched in every direction. All that could be seen in the distance were hills and trees.

"Rabbi Meir," said a young man with great respect, "you must be tired from the long walk we have taken today. I will run ahead and see if I can find the inn we heard about. Then I will come back with a horse for you to ride."

"Go, my son," said Rabbi Meir. The young man, Mordecai ben Hillel, set off. The aged Rabbi and the small group of followers sat down at the side of the road to wait.

Rabbi Meir was indeed tired. Over seventy years old, he had started out on a long and dangerous journey.

"It will be many days before we get to Italy," said a member of the group, as he rubbed his aching feet.

"And then we will have to find a ship that will take us across the Mediterranean Sea," said another.

The Hope of Syria

"We will find a ship," said Rabbi Meir. His voice was strong and confident, although he was old and weary. "We have been planning this for so long. The jewels we have hidden in our clothes will pay for our passage and for all we need."

"And then, freedom!" said the youngest traveler, the student Meir ha-Kohen. "We will be in the land of Syria, where Jews can live like human beings, without being afraid of the government or the Church. Think of it—and to be so close to the land of Israel, too!"

"Syria is also a land of the Bible," said

A Hebrew gravestone ot Germany of the time of Rabbi Meir.

Rabbi Meir. "There may come a time when God will call us from there to enter the Holy Land. We must wait for God's word."

"What kind of person do you think the adviser to the king of Syria is?" asked the student. "Some of us were wondering if he himself might be the Messiah."

Rabbi Meir shook his head. "We must not believe that the adviser to the Grand Khan is the Messiah," he said. "He is a man like ourselves. But God has helped him rise to a high office.

"The Grand Khan of Persia and Syria is not a Christian and not a Moslem; therefore he has no special love for either of those groups. He is a pagan, a Mongol from the Far East, who won the lands by war.

"When our beloved brother, the Jewish physician Saad Addaula, cured the Khan's illness, and gave him much good advice, the Khan made him his chief adviser and helper, and promised good treatment to any Jews who came into his kingdom."

The young student said thoughtfully, "It is good to know that there is one place in the world where the Jews don't have to keep paying tremendous taxes to the emperor, and the dukes, and the bishops, in order to have the privilege of staying."

"And where there is no danger of mobs rising up to burn Jewish books, as they did in Paris," said an older man, who was also a student of the Rabbi, "or take Jewish lives, as they have done in our own day in so many German cities."

One of the few women who had been brave enough to come on the journey was the wife of the student Mordecai. She spoke now, saying, "What we are doing now is most important. If our journey is successful, Jews from our cities and then from all over the world, all the Jews of the *Golah*, the Exile, will leave their homes and travel to Syria. There, when all the Jews are gathered and ready, the Messiah will come and lead us into the land of Israel."

Rabbi Meir did not correct the young woman, for the same hope was in all their hearts.

Meeting at the Inn

Just then a horse and rider appeared over the horizon. It was Mordecai returning.

"He has reached the inn and is returning to fetch us," said Rabbi Meir. " Our first day of travel is nearly over, and we are still safe."

At the same time as Rabbi Meir, riding slowly on the borrowed horse, with his followers walking on both sides, approached the inn, another group came up, from the opposite direction.

"Here are pilgrims returning from Italy," said the student Mordecai. "They can tell us how the roads are further south."

"Hold back," said Rabbi Meir. "Do not ask questions. It is better not to have much to say

to anyone, and not to let anyone know where we are going. You know there are those who would not want to let any Jews leave the country. They are afraid of losing our money and the taxes we pay."

The leader of the opposite group was looking at Rabbi Meir with curiosity. A person with him, dressed in a long cloak which he was raising to hide his face, was whispering to him and pointing towards the Jews.

Rabbi Meir was worried by this. "Let us enter the inn and go quickly to our rooms,"

A medieval drawing of a Hebrew teacher and his young pupil in Germany of the 13th century. Rabbi Meir was a more kindly teacher and had many students living in his own home.

he said.

The innkeeper had come out to greet the two bands of travelers. He turned towards the pilgrims from the south, and clapped his hands with delight.

Running over to the leader, he bowed and exclaimed, "Your Excellency, most reverend Bishop of Basel, I am so pleased that you will stop at my humble inn."

The Bishop did not smile, but frowned. He spoke rapidly to the innkeeper, who glanced round, called over a boy who worked for him, and sent him quickly on an errand.

The Bishop then approached the Rabbi. "Rabbi Meir of Rothenburg," said the churchman, in a loud voice. "Where do you think you and these other Jews are going?"

"How did he know who we are?" asked the

Rabbi's followers. Then the Rabbi saw the face of the Bishop's companion, who now was talking excitedly to the innkeeper.

"Alas and woe is to us," said the aged Rabbi. "I recognize that face. That man, may God forgive him, was a Jew in one of my early congregations, in the city of Nuremberg. He was always a strange person, without friends, and I heard later that he had forsaken his faith, and become a Christian. Now, in order to gain more favor with the Bishop, he has told him who we are. He has betrayed us."

The Bishop stood before the sad group of Jews. "The Chief Rabbi of Germany, such a rich and famous man, should not travel like a poor man with a crowd of beggars. It is a good thing I found out who you are, so you may receive an escort such as you deserve."

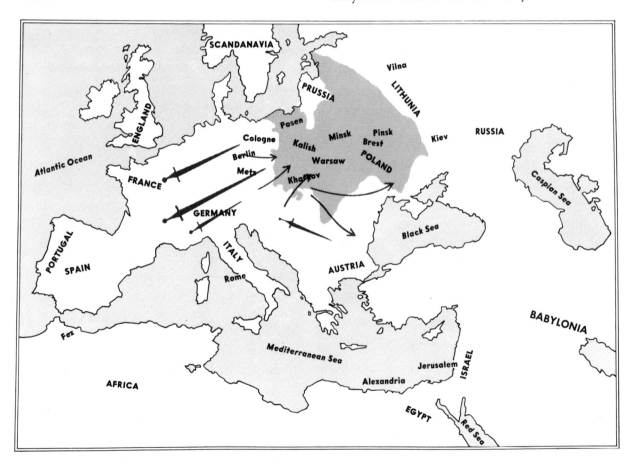

Persecutions and expulsions from German states 1350 to 1648. The many expulsions sent Jews eastward to Poland, where they were welcomed, and where they helped build up industry and trade.

The Arrest

The sarcastic remark of the Bishop had its meaning. In a few minutes, soldiers of the nearby Duke arrived and arrested the Rabbi for attempting to leave the country without permission. His followers watched in helpless grief.

Rabbi Meir did not give way to sorrow or fear. The old man stood erect, as the soldiers held him on either side.

"Do not weep, fellow Jews," he said. "This is God's doing. It is not yet time for the Jews to be gathered from their exile. Return to your homes."

"We will ransom you!" shouted Mordecai. "We will gather all the money they ask for, and buy you back from prison."

"No, no," said Rabbi Meir. "I beg of you. Do not pay for my release. Then the officials of every city will arrest rabbis and leading men, and ask for ransom. We cannot let the officials do this to our communities."

There was nothing further the Jews could do. They returned home broken-hearted. The journey had failed.

The soldiers took the aged scholar to the court of the Emperor Rudolph. The Bishop stood up as witness against the Rabbi.

"This Jew has conspired to leave his district and the noblemen to whom he owes loyalty. Not only that, but he has gathered followers to join him in leaving the country. They tried to smuggle out jewels with them, to cheat the emperor of taxes due to him."

"These are serious crimes," said the emperor. "Take this Rabbi to the prison tower. He must remain there for life."

The Rabbi held his head high. "This must be God's will," he said. "This may be the way I can best serve Him."

As the guards led the old man out, the emperor gave further instructions. "Treat him well," he said. "Rabbi Meir will be our hostage. While we hold their saintly leader in prison, no Jew in the country will try to leave, or will refuse to pay taxes."

A Scholar in Prison

Rabbi Meir was led to a room high in the prison tower. The guards had respect for this dignified scholar, and showed it in their courtesy to him.

"Why will you not eat the food we bring you?" asked the guard Ludwig, on the first day. "It is better than other prisoners get."

"I cannot eat food that is not kosher," answered the Rabbi.

"Where can we get food that is proper for you?" asked Ludwig.

"My friends and followers are waiting outside the tower compound," said the Rabbi. "If you will only allow them to enter, and talk this over with you, I think some arrangement can be made."

"This has never been done before," said Ludwig.

"If it cannot be done, it cannot be done," said Rabbi Meir. "Then I will live on water and fruit for as long as God wills it."

"The emperor said we should treat him well," said the second guard. "Let us talk to these Jews."

Not only did the Rabbi's loyal followers bring him food every day; they also were allowed to bring him books and writing materials, and to deliver and take letters. In the prison the Rabbi lived a Jewish life, though cut off from his people. He prayed and kept the Sabbath and holidays. His days were spent in study and writing.

In prison he wrote answers to questions of law sent to him from all over the world. He answered strictly in accordance with the laws of the Talmud. Just as he allowed himself no leeway in observance, even behind prison walls, so he expected all Jews to be faithful to the law. He continued writing Tosafot, additional commentaries on the Talmud.

When he was deep in study, or lost in the world of thought, Rabbi Meir forgot that he was in prison.

The Attempt at Ransom

In Rothenburg however, and the other cities of Germany, wherever Jews lived, there was distress over the plight of their leading Rabbi and sage. The Jews were helpless under the law of the land, for they had no rights in the courts.

As soon as the news of the Rabbi's imprisonment was heard, Jews both rich and poor crowded to the synagogue and studyhouse. "To redeem the Light of the Exile, *Me'or ha-Golah,* from captivity, we will give all our wealth," they promised.

Mordecai ben Hillel spoke to them, explaining, "The Rabbi has forbidden us to collect ransom money. He is afraid that many kidnapings and arrests of Jewish leaders will follow. Paying ransom will encourage such things; it will become a new way for the German authorities to make money."

"No, no, we must save the Rabbi!" came the cry. A poor widow brought a few copper coins; the wealthiest man poured silver. Young children helped to collect from every household.

In time, the great sum of 30,000 marks had been collected. A delegation of Jews went to the court of the emperor and informed him of what had been done.

Rabbi Meir Refuses

Ludwig the guard was happy. He had some good news for his prisoner. "Rabbi Meir, your God must have answered your prayers," he said. "Your people have come to the emperor today with 30,000 marks to buy your freedom."

"What do you say?" asked the Rabbi. In-

This Sabbath and festival lamp, made in Germany about 1710, was designed to be suspended from ceiling or wall.

stead of seeming pleased, he seemed dismayed. "This must never be. Tell the leaders of the Jewish community to release every giver from his pledge. The money must not be used."

The guard stared in amazement. "When your people love you so much as to gather this tremendous amount, a king's ransom, for you, do you mean to say you reject the offer?"

"I will never accept," said the Rabbi. "I will refuse to step forth from the tower. Tell them that if they have ever listened to my words, they must obey me now."

At last the people understood what Rabbi Meir meant: that the life of the Jews would be even more difficult if the emperor saw how much money they were willing to raise to redeem an imprisoned leader.

For seven years, the venerable rabbi lived in the prison. The Jews of Germany, France and Italy waited for his Responsa, his legal codes, and his poems, some of which were put into the prayerbook. Written in dismal prison surroundings, the poems show that the Rabbi kept alive his faith in God, in God's law, and in the coming of the Messiah—when God willed it.

The Rabbi and his followers had not been able to hasten the coming of the Messiah by traveling to Syria. But they kept faith in the justice of God. Ultimately, they knew, He would redeem Israel.

After seven years, the sad news came that the Rabbi had died, still in prison, a martyr to his love for his people. The Jews then had to pay a ransom, to gain permission to bury him in a Jewish cemetery.

The emperor may have thought he had won a victory. But even the guards in the tower could have told the emperor that the spirit of Rabbi Meir had won out, that nothing could overcome the pride and faith of such a man.

They had heard him say, and had seen proof of the saying in his life: "After a man has decided to give up his life to martyrdom, nothing further can hurt him. Imprisonment is sweet to a man if the truth is in prison with him."

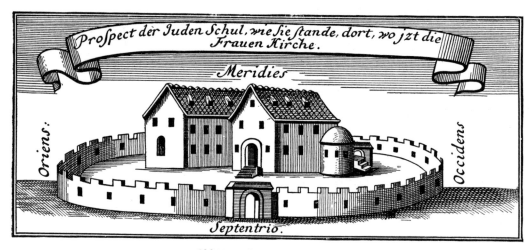

Old Nuremberg synagogue.

SOME RESPONSA OF RABBI MEIR

Question: A man died leaving a young son. Each one of the man's brothers demands that the orphan be left in his care.

Answer: The choice of the proper guardian for the child is not the responsibility of the brothers, but of the leaders of the community, who are the fathers of all orphans. Therefore, the elders of the community must decide on the proper guardian for the orphan.

*   *   *

Question: A tutor was hired for a season. He was ill part of the time and could not teach during that time. Should he be paid for the whole season?

Answer: There are laws in the Torah about the treatment of a slave; these also apply to a workman who was hired for a season. A slave who was sick for part of his six years of service does not have to make up for the time of his illness; he goes free at the end of the six years anyway. Similarly, the tutor should be paid for the entire season and does not have to make up for the time of his illness.

*   *   *

Question: What is the merit of going to live in the Holy Land?

Answer: There is a statement in the Talmud that one who goes to the Holy Land is considered free of sin. This refers to a man who commits no sins while he is in the Holy Land. The punishment for a sin committed there is worse than that for a sin committed elsewhere, for it is like a rebellion within the king's own palace. When a person goes to the Holy Land with sincere intentions and acts there with righteousness, his reward is great. He must, of course, be sure that he can support himself there.

*   *   *

Question: Why did the Amoraim remain in Babylonia?

Answer: If they had moved to the Holy Land, it would have meant an end to their studies, for they would have had to spend all their time trying to find a way to support themselves, since the land was desolate.

Isaac Abravanel

1437 - 1508

Every Purim, when we read the *Megillah,* the Book of Esther, we remember a question that Mordecai asked Queen Esther. When Esther at first hesitated about going to the king to save her people from Haman, Mordecai urged her, saying:

"Who knows if you were not raised to your royal position just for a time like this?"

Mordecai's words are a reminder to Jews who have become important or wealthy that they should not forget their people, but should use their power to help them.

One of the most faithful leaders the Jews ever had in the court of a king was Don Isaac Abravanel. He was born in Lisbon, the capital of Portugal, more than 500 years ago. Though at that time in Portugal, as well as in nearby Spain, the Jews had many enemies, Isaac Abravanel led for many years a happy and successful life.

Isaac's grandfather had come to Portugal from Spain. His father, Judah, was the treasurer in charge of all money matters for the king of Portugal. Young Isaac grew up in the court, wealthy and well-educated. He had as keen a mind as his father, and his noble character won him many friends.

A Favorite at Court

King Alfonso V in time appointed the younger Abravanel his treasurer. Isaac Abravanel's own words tell about his life at the court:

Tranquilly I lived in my inherited house in fair Lisbon. God had given me blessings, riches and honor. I had built myself stately buildings and chambers. My house was the meeting-place of the learned and the wise. I was a favorite in the palace of Alfonso, a mighty and upright king, under whom the Jews enjoyed freedom and prosperity. I was close to him, was his support, and while he lived, I frequented his palace.

Isaac Abravanel never forgot, however, that he was a Jew. He helped his people whenever he could. He was able to do much for them.

Once 250 Jews of Morocco were captured and sold as slaves. Abravanel wrote to important persons in every area where the slaves were sent. On his own, he collected a great sum of money, mostly from the Jews of Portugal, to buy back the unfortunate men and women. He was able to ransom and free every one of them.

His task did not stop there. Abravanel helped the Jewish community to support and teach the Moroccans until they were able to take their places in Portugal as free men.

His son wrote about him in later life: "He was a shield and a wall for his people, and delivered the sufferers from their oppressors."

King Alfonso always tried to be fair and kind to Isaac Abravanel's people. Abravanel often thanked him for not carrying out the cruel laws that would prevent the Jews from making a living and keeping their religion.

"As long as you are king," said Isaac Abravanel, "we Jews of Portugal have no fear."

"I will not be a king forever," good King Alfonso said, after many years of friendship with Isaac. "You know you have enemies. The time may come when the Jews, even you, may be in danger here. My heart aches when I think of the hardships that may befall you."

"Your majesty," said Isaac Abravanel, "I know you wish that I would give up my religion so that I might be safe from persecutors. But I would die rather than give up my faith."

The king sighed. "I knew you would say that," he said. "I respect you for it. But I fear for you."

Forced to Flee

The king's fears were well-founded. After his death, his best friends were accused of plotting against the new king. The Duke of Braganza, a friend of Abravanel, was hanged.

Isaac Aboab, rabbi of Amsterdam and the first rabbi in the Western hemisphere. In 1642 he was called to the Dutch Jewish colony of Recife in Brazil, but he returned to Amsterdam when the Portuguese conquered the colony in 1654 and introduced the Inquisition.

To save his own life. Isaac Abravanel was forced to leave house and fortune, and flee from the country where his family had lived in honor for generations.

Abravanel was able to find safety in Castile, a province of Spain. He arrived with his wife and sons in Toledo, where the Jews greeted him with joy. They were proud that such a famous and distinguished man had come to their community.

Rabbi Isaac Aboab, the leader of the Jewish community, saw to it that a home was found for Abravanel and his family, which included three young sons. On his first visit to the new home, the Rabbi found Isaac Abravanel surrounded by books, and busy writing.

"You are famous as a practical man who knows the ways of nations and kings," said the Rabbi. "I did not know you were so devoted to the holy books."

"I have studied all my life," answered Abravanel. "But affairs of the court took most of my time. Now I feel that in gratitude for my escape, I must give all my time to Torah. I am writing a commentary on the books of the Bible, starting with Joshua."

"Such a commentary is needed, Don Isaac," said the Rabbi. "Of the books of the Bible, the first five are studied and the others are often neglected. The later books need more attention."

Isaac Abravanel devoted himself for six months to his commentary. He wrote on the books of Joshua, Judges and Samuel. Now he was coming to the period of the kings of Israel and Judah. Abravanel could explain these books with unusual understanding, for no one knew more than he about the ways of kings and their courts.

But he was not able to continue his commentary on the Books of Kings until many years later, in another city. Instead, he again became part of a royal court.

The Court of Castile

Queen Isabella had heard with interest of the coming of Isaac Abravanel to her kingdom. She sent for him.

"Don Isaac," said the Queen, "you know that we are not fond of the Jews. We consider them mistaken in their religion, and will do all we can to show them the error of their ways.

"But you can be of use to us. We know the brilliant work you did for Alfonso. Now we appoint you to be chief of finance for our court."

Abravanel soon became as important in Castile as he had been in Portugal. He took

This Yom Kippur Mahzor, or prayer book, was a mute witness to the cruel period of the Inquisition in Spain and Portugal. It was designed in this elongated shape for a special purpose. In case of a surprise "visit" by officers of the government, Marrano Jews (who pretended to be Christians but who practiced Judaism secretly) would drop the prayer book into their wide sleeves and thus escape detection.

care of money matters for Isabella and her husband, King Ferdinand.

As court treasurer, Abravanel used his influence to help his people whenever he could. He tried to lower the heavy taxes the Jews had to pay. He tried to persuade Isabella not to support the church leaders who were carrying on the Inquisition.

The Terrors of the Inquisition

The Inquisition was an attempt to keep all Christians true to their church. Any unfortunate person who seemed to have the wrong beliefs, or who did not follow the rules of the Church in every way, could be arrested and brought to trial. Torture was used to make the prisoners confess.

Those who were considered guilty were further tortured and often executed, sometimes by being burnt at the stake. The executions were carried out by the government. Isabella always obeyed Tomás de Torquemada, the leader of the Inquisition. She felt she was being faithful to her religion by having the State obey the Church.

The Inquisition often arrested Jews, accus-ing them of trying to turn Christians from their faith.

The Marranos

There were also Marranos, secret Jews, who had been forced to pretend to become Christians. They kept Jewish law and studied Torah in secret, hoping for the time when they could be free Jews once more. If Marranos were discovered to be obeying Jewish law, torture and death were their fate. Their children were taken and given to strangers.

We know thousands of sad stories about the Marranos. We know how they used to hide their faces as they stole at night through the streets to a secret, dark cellar where they might pray once a year on *Yom Kippur*. The *Kol Nidre* prayer comforted them, for in it they asked that the false vows they had to take might be forgiven by God.

Marrano mothers, at night, behind locked windows, taught their children how to read the Hebrew prayers. On Friday evening they lit candles, sometimes in their basements, sometimes inside tall vases so no one could see the flames. They taught their daughters,

The golden tower at Seville, used as a residence by Jewish financiers of the kings of Castile.

whatever happened, to light two candles every Friday.

There are some Catholics today, in Spanish-speaking countries, who still have the custom of lighting candles on Friday. They do not know that their grandmothers and great-grandmothers continued to do this in memory of a promise made to a Jewish ancestor. Perhaps that ancestor had died at the stake, in an *Auto da Fe*, as the Church called it—an Act of Faith.

Abravanel found to his grief that he could do very little to change Isabella's mind. With bribes and pleas he was able to help only a few of his brothers who were caught by the Inquisition.

Money for War and for Exploration

Still Don Isaac was a powerful and important person at court.

When Castile carried on a war against Granada, it was Isaac Abravanel who was able to provide money for the conduct of the war. Whatever project the Queen had in mind, she turned to Abravanel for advice and for practical help.

One day there came a captain of a sailing ship to Isabella and Ferdinand.

"I have a plan," said the sailor, "that will bring great wealth to your majesty's court.

nnmer⁹ annornz	nomina menfinz	dies	digiti	feria	hore	minut	finis eclipfis hore	minu
Tab eclipfis luminariuz et primo de fole								
1493	octob	10	9	5	0	0	1	20
1502	feptēb	30	8	6	17	28	19	12
1506	Julii	20	3	2	1	49	3	3
K 13	martii	7	4	1	23	40	1	9
15 18	Junii	7	10	2	18	22	19	17
1524	fannaz	23	9	2	3	12	4	6
Tabla de eclipfib⁹ lune								
1494	feptēb	14	17	1	17	5	2	33
1497	fannaz	18	17	4	3	50	7	18
1500	nouēb	5	13	5	10	17	13	30
1501	maii	2	10	1	15	33	19	6
1502	octob	15	14	7	10	15	12	9
1504	febuā	20	16	5	10	47	14	13
1505	ang⁹	14	15	5	5	42	9	6
1508	Junii	12	23	2	15	21	19	0
1509	Junii	2	7	7	9	29	2	3
K 11	o:tob	6	13	2	9	11	2	25
15 14	fannaz	29	16	2	14	20	16	3
15 15	fannaz	19	15	7	5	0	6	42
15 16	Julii	13	14	1	10	0	12	30
15 19	nouēb	6	20	1	5	50	6	48

A chart from the *Almanach Perpetuum* of Abraham Zacuto, (Leiria, 1496).
Abraham Zacuto was a Spanish astronomer and Hebrew writer. Christopher Columbus used Zacuto's astronomical computations. Columbus learned from them of the moon's eclipse on February 29, 1504 (listed in the chart above), and used the information to overcome the hostility of the Indians on the Island of Jamaica.

The greatest demand all over Europe is for spices. All our ships have had to sail east to reach the land of India, to get these most expensive and desired items.

"I believe," the sailor went on, "that the world is round. None of our ships have dared to prove this, but I am willing.

"I will sail west, into the Ocean Sea. After a short voyage, according to my reckoning, I will reach the western coast of India. We will be able to reach India and China much more quickly and easily than those who sail east. The profit will be yours, and the glory of this great discoverey will be yours forever."

The man, of course, was Christopher Columbus. Isabella, after some consideration, was pleased to offer some support to the project.

To whom would Isabella turn to get the money for the three ships and all the supplies needed by Columbus? She could turn only to Isaac Abravanel, and to another Jew, Abraham Senior, who always found ways to borrow money for the Queen's expenses.

Much of the money for Columbus' first voyage must have come from the Jews. We know, also, that three of his crew, including Luis de Torres, the ship's doctor, were Marranos. De Torres was the first man of the Columbus's crew to set foot on American soil. Because he knew several languages, probably Hebrew, Aramaic, and Greek, he was sent ashore to talk to the Indians!

The Expulsion from Spain

At the time Columbus was gathering his ships and crew, Abravanel and the Jews received a terrible blow, which made them forget everything else.

Torquemada, the fanatical chief of the Inquisition, could no longer stand having the Jews defy him. He came to Isabella.

"The presence of Jews is an insult to us and to our Lord," he said. "If you want to be true to your Church, you must issue a decree: Either the Jews become Christians, or they must leave! Let no Jew remain in your kingdom!"

Isabella listened meekly, as she always did. The decree went forth. The Jews were given a few months to make up their minds. By July 31 of 1492, they had to decide.

Jews had been living in Spain for 1500 years. They knew no other country; this was their home. Among the Jews had been scholars, poets, physicians, philosophers, some of the greatest minds in the history of Spain. They had given much to the glory of their country.

Now they were faced with the choice of leaving their faith or leaving their country. They faced Exile in poverty, for they were not allowed to take property with them.

Isaac Abravanel did his utmost. With great effort he gathered a tremendous sum of money, 30,000 ducats. He offered it to Isabella and Ferdinand if they would take back the cruel edict.

Ferdinand knew that the court always needed money to carry on its wars and its luxuries. He might have been willing to accept the payment.

But Isabella was too much under the influence of Torquemada. She would not change her decision.

The Jews had to leave. The only allowance that was made was that they might leave two days later than July 31.

The Saddest Day

The date on which they left thus fell on the ninth day of the Hebrew month of Av. This was the fast-day of *Tishah b'Av*, the day on which we remember two other disasters in the history of our people, the destruction of the First and then of the Second Temple.

The despair of the exiled Jews is impossible for us to imagine. The wandering and poverty they faced, their fears for themselves and their children, the danger of sea-voyages in rickety, overcrowded ships, might have made them turn back. But they did not turn back.

They wept goodbye to their homes, their country, the graves of their ancestors, and set out to an unknown fate, rather than give up their religion.

Some went to Portugal, some to Italy, some to North Africa, some to Holland. For many of them, their worst fears were realized. They were lost on the way or sold as slaves. Thousands were stricken with the plague.

Everywhere they landed, Jews tried to help them. There was great respect for these proud, faithful, and learned Spanish Jews.

Other Cities and a New Land

Isaac Abravanel went into exile with his people. He was one of those who found a safe haven, in the Italian city of Naples. Again his fame had gone before him. He entered the service of the king of Naples, and later of the king's son, Alfonso II. In his position, Abravanel was able to help many of his fellow refugees find homes and employment.

But the French attacked Naples, and Abravanel fled with the king. First in one city, then in another, Don Isaac remained active in court and state affairs. His last position was in the court of Venice. There he completed his commentary on the Bible. His sons became poets and physicians, respected and honored.

In his old age, Isaac Abravanel was weary of his wanderings and broken-hearted at the sufferings of his people, of which he had seen so much. All his life he had helped them as much as he could. As he looked around, he could see that the position of the Jews was no better. Like himself, many of the Jews had to flee from one country to another, never finding peace. The only hope, he wrote, was the coming of the days of the Messiah.

There was another hope, however, for the Jews, something Isaac Abravanel did not even realize. On the day of the Expulsion from Spain, August 2, 1492, when thousands of weeping Jews set out on their sad journeys, the three ships of Columbus also left the Spanish harbor.

In the voyages of Columbus, and his opening of the New World, lay the promise that the Jews would someday find a home where they could live freely and proudly.

Isaac Abravanel had a share in this great adventure. In a life devoted to his faith and his people, he had unknowingly helped grant the Jews, and all the world, a new hope of freedom.

פירוש נביאים אחרונים

מחבר הרב הגדול שלשלת היחס נודע בשערים שמו הדון

דון יצחק אברבנאל

נדפס שנת

Title page of the commentary of Don Isaac Abravanel to the "Later Prophets."

SELECTIONS FROM ISAAC ABRAVANEL

When I lived in royal courts, I had hardly any time to spend on books. It was only after I became an exile and a wanderer in the world, going penniless from kingdom to kingdom, that I became a student of the Holy Book.

* * *

What can be the reward of souls in the World to Come? It will be that they will reach a true understanding of God, which will give them the most wonderful joy, something a man cannot arrive at in this life.

* * *

Only a man whose thoughts are pure, who keeps far from sin, and who is humble and modest, deserves to be king.

* * *

God does not want us to be ascetics, to keep away from all pleasure and good things of the world. The law tells us to keep the middle way. Long fasting is not a pious act for a person who does not even desire food. One should not feel that it is wrong to have wealth, if it is gained in a proper way, and if it does not interfere with study and good deeds.

* * *

The righteous man is like a prince, a ruler of a kingdom, who is obeyed by his servants, that is, his senses and his desires, his mental and physical faculties, which he governs. He controls his passions, keeping them within limits, and at the same time giving them their share in order to satisfy them, just as a prince controls his subjects. If he has satisfied each of them (giving to his bodily servants the necessary amount of food, cleanliness, and rest; waking, exercise, and worldly occupation), he can call upon his community as a respected prince calls his disciplined army, to assist him in gathering the highest goals.

Joseph Caro

1488 - 1575

On the deck of one of the crowded ships leaving the shore of Spain on the tragic day of the Expulsion in 1492, stood a small family. The mother was crying so much she could not speak. The father lifted up his little son.

"Look, Joseph, look at Spain. Say goodbye to our home."

The little boy struggled to get down from his father's arms. "It's not fair," he shouted. "God won't let them be so cruel to us."

The father put the boy down and said sadly, "When God is ready, He will send the Messiah to save us. Till then, all we can do is hope and pray."

The child stared back into his father's eyes. "I won't wait till God is ready," he said. "It's been too long. I want to make the Messiah come right away."

Hearing this, the mother stopped crying, and exclaimed, "Joseph, you must not say such a thing! It's a sin to think we can make God do what we want."

The father was not so distressed. "He's only a little child, Rachel. God will forgive him. And maybe, who knows, maybe our Joseph will do great things . . ."

Dreams of Greatness

Ephraim Caro and his wife and son settled in the city of Nicopolis in Turkey, where the father was respected as a teacher of Talmud.

As the boy Joseph grew up, he heard many stories of the sufferings of his people. A silent child, who devoted himself to books, he would clench his fists and grit his teeth, but he never again shocked his mother by saying he would bring the Messiah.

Instead, he did as his parents wished him to, and studied all day and far into the night. Even his proud father was amazed at the progress of his son's learning. At an early age, Joseph had memorized the entire six books of the Mishnah.

In secret, Joseph imagined doing all sorts of things to save his people. He, Joseph Caro, might be the leader who would unite all Israel and bring the Messiah down to earth.

As a grown man, known as the leading scholar of his country, and married to the daughter of a great Talmudist, Joseph Caro continued to dream.

Long and lonely hours of study began to give him strange ideas. He imagined that the Mishnah itself became a kind of holy messenger, an angel who would tell him what to do. The messenger told him, he thought, to eat and drink little, to devote himself to study and prayer, and prepare himself for a great life and death that would save his people.

The Kabbalah

In his search for instruction, Joseph Caro turned to books other than the Bible and the Talmudic writings. There were other works which tried to answer questions that people have always asked: What is life's meaning; how and for what purpose were the world and man created; how may man best serve God and come near to Him in holiness; why and for how long were the Jews doomed to suffer in exile; and when might man hope for the coming of redemption.

These writings, the work of men called mystics who devoted thmselves to the soul and its relationship to God, form the body of tradition known as Kabbalah.

The most important book of Kabbalah is the Zohar, a book produced by Moses de Leon about 1400. It was supposed to be the hidden work of the saintly Simon bar Yohai, who had died more than a thousand years before in Palestine.

Through study of the Zohar, Joseph Caro tried to find how to bring redemption to the Jews. He was helped in his search by a most unusual companion who came to study with him.

אני דויד בן המלך שלמה

[handwritten letter in Hebrew]

A letter of David Reubeni, claiming that he represented a Jewish kingdom in the desert.

Solomon Molko

In Portugal lived a handsome and brilliant young man, raised as a Christian, well-educated and serving as a court secretary. The young man, Diogo Pires, had been told that his parents were Marranos, secret Jews, who had brought him up as a Christian so that his life might be safe from the Inquisition, which had spread to Portugal.

A Jewish traveler, David Reubeni, came to his city and spoke to small groups of Marranos, trying to give them hope for the future. As he spoke, young Diogo was inspired. He felt that he was receiving the word of God, telling him he must become a Jew once more, and sacrifice himself for his people.

Taking the name of Solomon Molko, the young man gave up his own safety and security, and traveled as a Jew to Italy, to Turkey, and to the city of Safed in Palestine.

He had, it was said, the face and voice of an angel, and charmed his listeners, so that Christians not only left him unharmed, but listened in fascination to his words. The Pope himself gave him an audience, and found himself listening to a plea to stop the Inquisition.

When Solomon Molko came to Adrianople in Turkey, he was met by the scholar Joseph Caro. The fiery young man had a strong influence on Caro, whose thoughts were tending in the same direction, towards the miraculous saving of the Jewish people. Together they studied and found inspiration in the pages of the Zohar.

Joseph Caro and Solomon Molko decided finally that the Messiah would come when the

The scene of an Auto-da-Fe. The crowd seems to enjoy the executions.

Jewish people were united in keeping the Torah, under the leadership of a rabbi ordained in the land of Israel.

A Martyr to His Faith

Leaving Joseph Caro, Solomon Molko continued his journeys, proclaiming that he was God's messenger, and announcing that the Messiah was soon to come.

In Italy, the Emperor Charles decided that an end had to be put to the activities of the strange and daring young man. He had Solomon Molko arrested and sentenced to death at an *Auto da Fe*. He was to be burned alive at the stake in the public square of Mantua.

The emperor had heard about the strange power the young man had over those who listened to him. He himself refused to meet Solomon Molko, and he gave special instructions to the executioners:

"Do not look at the prisoner's face, and do not allow him to speak to you or the crowd."

To make sure he would not speak, the guards gagged him before bringing him to the square. At the stake, at the very last minute, the emperor came forward, looked into the prisoner's eyes, and said, "Sinner as you are, you are too young to die. Will you not give up your unholy faith, return to the Church, and throw yourself upon our mercy?"

The executioner removed the gag.

"I will die a Jew," said Solomon Molko. "This is what I knew my end would be. I have had visions of this day for many years. I will have the glory of being consumed on the altar as a holy sacrifice."

Before the emperor and the disbelieving crowd, Molko was burnt at the stake, his faith unshaken.

"I, too, should show my love for God by dying for my faith," lamented Joseph Caro when he heard of the death of his friend. But this was not to be. Instead, he showed his love

Colophon on the last page of *The Orah Hayyim*, printed by Abraham Conat, 1476.

for Judaism and for God through years of studying, teaching and writing.

A Code of Jewish Law

Joseph Caro journeyed to Palestine, becoming a member of the group of scholars at Safed who studied Talmud and Kabbalah, and prayed for the coming of the Messiah.

In his mind was always the desire to unify the Jewish people under one law.

The many Jews who traveled from one country to another found that customs might be different from the ones they had followed at home. Though the basic laws were the same, it might be the custom in one town to stand while saying a certain prayer; in another, to sit. In one city a special fast day might be kept, and not in another. Some communities might allow the eating of certain foods on Passover that others would not.

When questions of law arose, the Jews turned to the Codes, organized collections of the laws of the Rabbis. Joseph Caro devoted much time and thought to the Codes, writing a tremendous commentary on the most famous Code, the Turim.

He then decided he would have to produce a real guidebook, a simple, well-ordered collection of laws that would answer every question for "young students," as he said, who might not be able to use his commentary. He would include every law and custom that a Jew had to follow. Different subjects would be in different chapters.

The Shulhan Arukh

Because of his careful arrangement of the laws, he called his work the Shulhan Arukh, or "The Set Table." In it he included laws for the life of the Jew from the time he woke up in the morning till he fell asleep at night. He gave laws in the smallest detail on how to prepare kosher food; how to keep the Sabbath and holidays; how to pray; how to fulfill all ritual laws; how to live a good life. There are many statements on being a good neighbor, avoiding gossip, and being kind and merciful.

All mitzvot, all religious commandments, were to be performed with a joyful heart as a service to God.

Caro's works were read by all the Jewish communities of the world. The Jews of Italy, where printing flourished, collected money to print the commentaries and the Shulhan Arukh. Joseph Caro was the most famous scholar since the time of Maimonides.

Not all Jews, however, agreed with every word in the Shulhan Arukh. In countries to the north, great scholars held some different opinions from those of the Sephardi sage, Joseph Caro.

Title page of an early edition of the Shulhan Arukh, which was first published in 1564.

"If Joseph Caro calls his work a Table," said the learned Moses Isserles, "I will provide a Tablecloth."

That is just what he did. He wrote a commentary on the *Shulhan,* and called it the *Mapah,* or Tablecloth. The Jews of the northern and eastern countries of Europe, called Ashkenazi Jews, never studied one without the other.

Joseph Caro did not, therefore, succeed in making all the Jews of the world follow one rabbi and obey the laws in the exact same way. The Shulhan Arukh in its many volumes is, however, the most widely used guide to Jewish laws. It is still studied today by those who want to answer questions about preparing food, praying, mourning, keeping holidays—all the forms and rituals of Jewish life.

A much simpler form of the Shulhan Arukh, the *Kitzur* or shortened version, has been translated into English for use by less learned Jews.

Joseph Caro did not see the fulfillment of his lifelong dream and dearest wish—to see the Jewish people united under one leadership, and so to bring nearer the days of the Messiah. Yet, although the Messiah did not appear, the Jewish people managed to live on. Surely Joseph Caro's work, teaching the Jews how to keep the laws of their religion, was a great force of survival. In a way, he did help bring about a miracle: the survival of the Jewish people through their persecutions.

Joseph Caro's efforts to make his people better Jews earn for him the praise contained in one of his own favorite sentences from the Talmud:

"Whoever teaches others to do good is even greater than the doer."

SELECTIONS FROM THE SHULHAN ARUKH

"I have set the Lord always before me." This sentence from the Psalms *tells us how to act at all times. The way a person acts when alone in his house is not the same as in the presence of a great king. In the company of a king, a man would surely be careful of his actions and consider well what he says. So much the more should a man be careful in his actions when he considers that the Great King, the Holy One, always stands near him and watches what he does.*

* * *

When a man has a mezuzah *on his doorpost, every time he comes in or goes out he will see it, will remember that God's name is written in it, and will be reminded to obey the laws and be a righteous person.*

* * *

It is the nature of man to follow his friends and neighbors in his actions; therefore he should try to associate with good and wise people, and keep far away from the wicked, so that he should not learn their deeds. In Proverbs *it is written: "He that walketh with wise men will become wise; but he that walks with fools will be destroyed."*

* * *

If you want to take vengeance on your enemy, then become a fine and good person, whom everyone admires and speaks well of, for this way your enemy will be annoyed when he hears words of praise spoken of you. But if you want to make your enemy happy, then do wrong things, and he will rejoice over your disgrace and shame.

* * *

When a man is engaged in business or labor in order to make a living, he should not be interested in getting more and more money for the sake of the wealth alone. He should keep in mind that his aim is to support his family, to give charity, and to raise his children for the study of the Torah, so that they may be righteous and a credit to him and to their people.

* * *

It is written: "Remember the Sabbath day to keep it holy." One should prepare the best meat, fish, dessert and good wine, as well as one can afford, for the Sabbath. The silverware in the house should be polished in honor of the Sabbath and fresh coverings should be put on the beds; one should use one's best dishes, and the table should be covered with a cloth the entire day. One should try to wear fine clothes in honor of the Sabbath, not the same as those worn on weekdays. One should bathe before the Sabbath. One should think over the deeds of the past six days on the day before the Sabbath, and resolve to correct past mistakes and to do better in the week to come. One should rejoice with the coming of the Sabbath. If the coming of a distinguished guest would make one set his house in order and prepare the best of everything, how much more so the coming of Queen Sabbath.

UNIT FOUR

BEGINNINGS OF THE MODERN AGE

The end of the Middle Ages is called the period of the Renaissance (a French word meaning "rebirth"). It is described as a time of new ideas and new ways of living, a time of more freedom and more self-expression for the individual. In the Europe of the Middle Ages, all men were expected to belong to the one Church, to obey authority, and to remain in the condition of life to which they were born. Beginning about 1450 there came a period of exploration and discovery, commerce and wealth, art and learning. Men were inclined to think for themselves. National boundaries and the social order were changed.

It was not a time of more freedom for the Jews. On the contrary, it was just this period that saw the growth of *ghettos,* sections of cities where Jews were required to live in Italy, Germany, and other countries. They were not allowed to leave except at certain times, and were thus separated from the Christian community in every way. Some ghettos were walled and had guards standing at the entrances. It is no wonder that the Jews of the ghettos felt like outcasts from society, and were looked on as inferior by the rest of the population.

The Jews, crowded together in their small area, lived according to their own laws and standards. They celebrated their holidays like one family, and educated their children and took care of their needy without help from the outside.

THE PROTESTANT REFORMATION

It might have been thought that at a time of change and reform, when the Church of Rome itself was under attack, the Jews might benefit by a lessening of persecution. Indeed, when the great rebellion against the Catholic Church took place in the sixteenth century, it seemed for a while as though better times were coming.

The single narrow street of an Italian ghetto.

Martin Luther, the German monk who protested against the evils of the Church (1520) and became the founder of Protestant Christianity, at first spoke kindly to the Jews. He objected to the harshness of Church rule and to the fact that the Church was too wealthy and powerful. He wanted to go back

Martin Luther, leader of the Reformation.

to individual study of the Bible, instead of having priests explain everything to the people. He spoke against oppression of the Jews.

All this made him seem a just and liberal person. Soon, however, Luther realized that his kindness was not making the Jews join his religious movement. They still remained loyal to their own faith. Luther then became an enemy of the Jews.

At the same time, the original Church, now called the Roman Catholic Church, tried to strengthen itself against the inroads of the new movement, and became harsher than before to "Jews and heretics."

Protestantism spread to many countries of Europe, making most headway in the northern lands that were farther away from Rome. In England, King Henry VIII broke with Rome, proclaiming himself the head of the Church of England. Denmark, Norway, Sweden, Switzerland, and Holland became largely Protestant.

Soon there erupted religious wars between Protestant and Catholic kingdoms. In France there was civil war between the two factions, until Protestants were allowed their freedom.

The Thirty Years War (1618-1648) was between Protestant princes and the Catholic emperor of the "Holy Roman Empire"—the name given to the loose grouping of Germanic states. Eventually, the Catholic rulers of France joined on the Protestant side; and the Hapsburg family, rulers of Germany, were defeated. It can be seen by the final action that it was not really Protestants against Catholics, but nations against each other. Now religious differences helped to strengthen each country's patriotism, and its hatred of its enemies. There was no longer a single Church to unify Europe.

SOME LANDS OF FREEDOM

The free spirit of the new age showed itself in a good way in Holland, and then in England. While the Jews of most of Europe were in their ghetto-prisons, the small brave country of Holland permitted the Marranos who had escaped to its shores to practice their Judaism openly. The Jews were able to establish synagogues and join in trade, even traveling to the Dutch colonies across the sea in North and South America.

The freedom the Jews enjoyed in Amsterdam was proven by the life of Baruch or Benedict Spinoza (1632-1677), a Sephardi Jew who left the religious community. He became a freethinking philosopher, associating with Christians who also were not orthodox in their beliefs. Though he questioned the Bible and did not keep Jewish law, he believed everything in the world showed God's presence. He stressed ethics and good behavior, as one might expect from his early Jewish training.

An outstanding member of the Amsterdam Jewish community was Menasseh ben Israel (1604-1657), rabbi, teacher, writer and printer. He was interested in America, and wrote that the American Indians must be the descendants of the Lost Ten Tribes of Israel.

Menasseh ben Israel never crossed the Atlantic to America, but he did succeed in crossing the Channel to England. Since 1290 no Jew had a legal right to live there. Oliver Cromwell was now (1655) ruling England. He was interested in the possible return of the Jews for two reasons. One was that he saw the Jews had done much to make Holland prosperous. The other was that he was a religious Christian, and believed an idea that Menasseh ben Israel proposed: It would only be when the Jews were scattered to every nation of the world (this, of course, would have to include England) that the Messiah would come.

Cromwell was not able to pass a law stating that Jews were welcome to England. There would have been much opposition to such a law. However, a national conference discussed the matter, without coming to a definite conclusion. Gradually Jewish merchants began to enter England. When King Charles was restored to the throne a few years later, the presence of Jews was taken for granted.

JEWS IN AMERICA

Jews had settled in the new lands of America almost from the beginning. They had gone for the most part to Spanish, Portuguese and Dutch colonies in Mexico and South and Central America, many of them as Marranos.

When the Dutch conquered the Portuguese colony of Recife, in Brazil, the Marranos there immediately became Jews once more. They even invited (1642) a rabbi from Amsterdam, Isaac Aboab da Fonseca. Unfortunately, the Portuguese reconquered the colony and introduced the Inquisition.

Twenty-three of the Jews who escaped from Recife sailed first to the West Indies and then, in a small boat, the *Saint Charles,* to the Dutch colony in North America. They landed in the port of New Amsterdam in September 1654. Peter Stuyvesant, the governor, wished to turn them away. They were penniless, not even able to pay for their voyage. Further, Stuyvesant did not even want Catholics, or Protestants who did not belong to the Dutch Reformed Church, to settle in his colony. How could he allow Jews? He wrote a complaint to the Dutch West India Company.

Two of the Jews were put in prison as hostages for their debt. The others managed to survive with some help from the Dutch settlers. Finally the answer to Peter Stuyvesant's letter came back from the home base in Amsterdam. It told him that there were Jews among the owners of the company. It further reminded him that these refugees had fought for Holland in South America. Stuyvesant was forced to allow the Jews to stay.

A letter of the Jews of London to Oliver Cromwell, dated March 24, 1655, pleading that "we may with security meet privately in our particular houses for our devotions."

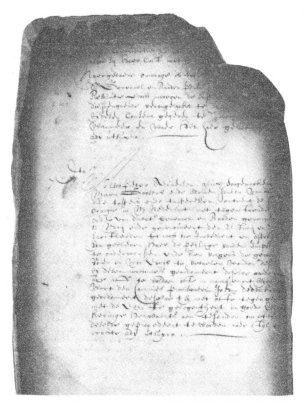

First entry in the Dutch records of New York City relating to the Jews, Sept. 7, 1654.

There still remained a struggle for civil rights. The Jews fought for the right to build a synagogue. This was not granted for some time, but they were allowed to worship in a private home. Their most aggressive member, Asser Levy, insisted on the right to stand guard in the colony like any citizen, instead of paying a tax. In ten years, when the British took over the colony and named it New York, the Jews were enjoying many rights of citizenship.

THE MOVE TO EASTERN EUROPE

The numbers of Jews who found homes in these lands of freedom were few. The greatest number of Jews, and the most important center of learning, were to be found in Eastern Europe, the countries of Poland and Lithuania. When the community of Spain had been destroyed, and the community of Germany and France was being weakened by constant oppression, the East European settle-

ment had grown and established itself.

Boleslav, one of the first rulers of Poland, had invited Jews to enter his territory as early as 1264. The Slavic tribes who lived in the area were not as advanced as the peoples of Western Europe. Boleslav and, later, King Casimir the Great of Poland, were glad to welcome Jews from the highly civilized countries of the west. The Jews developed industry and carried on trade, helping the country to become established. There were even coins minted by Jewish merchants, bearing Hebrew letters.

Other Jews came from southern countries, and a large community grew up. Given much freedom, the Jews conducted their business according to Talmudic law, and developed their own community organization. The Jewish community in each town was called the *Kahal.* It had its president; its *gabbaim,* or trustees; its charity funds, synagogue, baths, hospital, orphans' home, or whatever was needed. The Jews collected their own taxes and dealt with civil matters in their own courts.

By the sixteenth century, great Jewish communities had been established in Poland and Lithuania. The Crusades, the persecutions at the time of the Black Death, wars and oppression and expulsion had sent many Jews from Germany to these countries. With them the Jews had brought their culture and love of learning.

Now it was the Slavic lands that had the great talmudical academies. Every young man was expected to attend such a school, called a *yeshiva.* There was no question that every child was taught to read and write, though such a situation was far from true of the gentile population around them. Beyond that, almost the entire population went on to study even through the adult years.

The Talmud, by which, indeed, the life and even the business matters of the people

A typical Heder of the city of Vilna.

were regulated, was the subject of study. Every commentary on the Talmud was considered important and valuable. If different commentators seemed to disagree on their explanation of a sentence, the students would exercise their minds to solve the difficulty. Keen reasoning was used to show that the seeming contradiction could be explained away. This method of study was called *pilpul*.

The high level of learning among the entire population was never equalled by any previous community, Jewish or non-Jewish. Torah was in truth their life and the length of their days.

THE YIDDISH LANGUAGE

Jews had always spoken the language of the lands they lived in. Maimonides spoke and wrote in Arabic; Rashi spoke French. In Germany the Jews had spoken German. Of course, they all knew Hebrew, and in their speech at home they would also use some Hebrew phrases, or Aramaic words from the Talmud. In Eastern Europe, the language of the Jews was Yiddish.

When the Jews became more and more cut off from their neighbors, their language became more and more their own. The Jews of Poland brought with them the German that was spoken in their previous home. Through the centuries it developed, and more Hebrew and occasionally Polish and other words from their new neighbors were mixed in. This language of the Jews, called *Yiddish,* is basically German and can be largely understood by a modern speaker of German, but the pro-

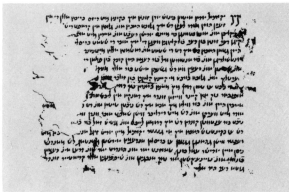

A promissory note in Yiddish, dated 1435.

nunciation and some of the words are different.

Yiddish was written and printed in Hebrew letters, for of course these were the letters that every Jew learned. It is interesting that Sephardi Jews, those from Spanish-speaking countries, developed a language called *Ladino,* easily recognized as Spanish in origin, and also written in Hebrew letters.

"Der Jude." Front page of a German-Jewish weekly.

Although Jews all over the world, in every century, have learned Hebrew, there are of course many Jewish groups from Sephardi or Eastern communities, who never had any reason to know Yiddish. Still Yiddish has been the most truly Jewish language to grow up outside of Israel. It has been spoken by millions of Jews, and its literature has expressed the finest and deepest feelings of the Jewish people.

DISASTER STRIKES

Poland had conquered and ruled the Ukraine, a southern Russian territory. The Polish landlords were cruel and took heavy taxes. Unfortunately, the landowners often put Jews in charge of collecting taxes from the people. The Ukrainians, hating their Polish rulers, also hated the Jews.

An officer of the Ukrainian army, named Chmelnitzki, led a rebellion against Poland (1648). His followers were cruel, hard-riding Cossacks. Bands of Tatars joined them, and they overran Poland. Poles and Jews were killed or sold into slavery. When this invasion was ended, Sweden and Russia both attacked Poland.

After ten years of war, Poland had driven out her enemies. Although the Jews had lost at least 100,000 lives and had been left destitute, the Poles were not friendly towards them. There were *pogroms,* riots against the Jews by their own neighbors.

FALSE MESSIAHS

At such a time, there seemed to be no hope for the future. The Jews turned more to the study of Kabbalah, hoping desperately that the terrible events they had gone through were the evil times that were supposed to come right before the Messiah's arrival. Things were so bad that they could not get worse; they looked for a miraculous deliverance.

With such preparation, a handsome young man by the name of Sabbetai Zevi was able to gain many followers when he announced he was the Messiah. He had come from Turkey, traveled to Cairo, gained support of a wealthy Jew there, and announced his mission in Jerusalem. Mystics of the Holy Land believed in him. In Cairo he gained a strong following.

Soon word of a Messiah had spread through Europe. There was a frenzy of acceptance. Intelligent people prepared to follow the Messiah to Palestine, some even selling their homes and possessions.

Sabbetai went to Constantinople, where he said he would become king. He was arrested there by Turkish authorities. Jews still believed in him. Finally he was brought before the Sultan. To save his life, Sabbetai Zevi gave up all his claims, and agreed to become a Moslem.

The shock of this terrible disappointment

An artist's fanciful view of the false Messiah, Sabbetai Zvi.

can hardly be imagined. Some followers could not bear it, but insisted that Sabbetai had gone into hiding, and was still the Messiah. They waited for a second coming. For generations afterwards, there was one after another who said he was the son or representative of Sabbetai, or that he himself was the Messiah. The people still longed for miracles to save them from their difficult and miserable lives.

HASIDISM

An answer to the needs of the people was found in the great movement of Hasidism. Israel ben Eliezer, a pious Jew of a small town in Poland, began to teach the joy and fulfilment of a life of love for God. He taught that God loved all men, poor as well as rich, unlearned as well as scholars; that God valued the heart of man, and that feeling and devotion in prayer, and service of God through joy, were what He desired.

Israel, called the *Baal Shem Tov,* or Master of the Good Name, brought brightness into the gloom that had fallen over the Jews of his time. He gave hope and self-respect to the least important Jew. His followers soon numbered in the thousands. They were called *Hasidim,* Pious Ones.

In Hasidic thought, the *Tzaddik,* or truly righteous man, was the one to help the people reach true understanding and closeness to God. The Baal Shem was the first Tzaddik. After his death there arose many more such leaders. They were called by the name *Rebbe;* and each group of Hasidim was guided by its own Rebbe.

Shneur Zalman of Ladi was a Rebbe who stressed the need for mind as well as heart, for learning as well as devotion. The movement in Hasidism which he started is known as *Habad,* after the first letters in the Hebrew words for Wisdom, Understanding, and Knowledge.

THE GAON OF VILNA

The Hasidic movement spread widely, but was stopped in most of Lithuania and nearby areas by the influence of Elijah, the great scholar called the Gaon of Vilna. He saw that the followers of the movement were breaking with authority, were developing customs of their own, and were discouraging intense study of the Talmud. A man who hardly ever made any public statements, he felt he had to speak against Hasidism.

The Gaon spent his whole life in study. He cut through the layers of commentary to come to the basic meaning of the words of the Talmud. His method of study, pure and scientific, helped to prepare the way for broader culture and a modern outlook. After his death, his ideas were carried on in the Yeshiva of Volozhin.

MOSES MENDELSSOHN

Meanwhile, in Germany, the small Jewish community that remained was confined to certain towns and ghetto areas, and cut off from all rights of citizenship. The man who helped most to gain respect for the Jews was Moses Mendelssohn. Completely self-educated, he rose to become a leading philosopher and writer, admired by all of Germany.

Mendelssohn wanted his people to become cultured and educated, so that they could be accepted in German society. He tried to teach them good German by translating the Bible into that language. He explained his religion as a way of life based on law, saying that there were no required beliefs or dogmas in Judaism.

In all his efforts to gain civil rights for the Jews, he warned that if they had to give up their religion in order to enter society, they should rather give up the privileges of citizenship. He wanted his people to remain faithful and proud Jews.

The eighteenth century was a time when men thought boldly, used their minds and developed new ideas. The century ended in revolutions, the American and the French. The bells ringing for freedom sounded a note of hope for the Jews of the modern world.

Israel Baal Shem Tov

1700 - 1760

Two young students of the Talmud, as might be seen at any school of Eastern Europe.

Six days a week, early in the morning, even before the sun was up in winter, the children in a little Polish town would walk down the muddy streets towards their *Heder,* the one-room school where the *Rebbe* would teach them Torah.

Every morning except *Shabbat,* the young students, some of them only four or five years old, would yawn and rub their eyes as they walked, and drag their feet slowly along the way.

The busy housewives cleaning their homes, and the men getting ready to say morning prayers, would look out to see the children as they passed.

One morning, a strange thing happened. The children, instead of shuffling along, were marching happily. They were singing and swinging their arms as they walked. Gay tunes that were usually heard only on *Simhat Torah* filled the air.

"What is it? Who has done this?" one neighbor asked another.

The answer came back, "It is Israel, the Orphan. He is now the helper who brings the little ones to school. He is teaching the children to sing."

Israel the Orphan

Everyone knew Israel, the son of Eliezer.

He was at this time only twelve years old himself, but he had been appointed to the job of helping the youngest students. It was not because he was the best boy in the class. It was because the community had taken care of him since the death of his parents, and it was thought he could do some work to earn his keep.

"I'm not sure it's a good idea," said Sarah to her neighbor Leah as they washed their clothes at the river. "He is an odd boy, always has been. He sings, he talks to himself, he runs off for hours to play by himself in the woods. Maybe he will be a bad influence on the little ones."

"Poor boy," said Leah. "He is an orphan. True, the town takes care of him: we give him clothes and food. But he has no parents to care for him. We must forgive him if he acts a little strange."

Indeed, Israel took good and loving care of the children. The love in his heart found an answer in theirs. Israel was not strict with them, like their teachers and parents.

On the way to Heder, he might stop. "Hush. Listen to the little bird singing." As the children for the first time became aware of the bird, Israel would tell them, "The little creature is full of joy. His song is a prayer of thanksgiving to God."

In the spring, he would show them a new bud on a tree. "See how God gives life. Everything created by God has some of His holiness in it."

The children would open their eyes wide. They knew that God had given the Torah. They knew that God was the Judge of the earth. But they had never thought of seeing God's love in a bird or a tree.

In time, the leaders of the community appointed the orphan Israel ben Eliezer to the position of *Shammash* of the synagogue. He took care of the books, called men to worship, and welcomed the wanderers who slept in the synagogue because they had no place else to go.

After a few years, Israel left his town and himself became a wanderer. Sometimes he taught children in one community or another. He lived sometimes with peasants on farms or in the woods, often dressing in the rough jacket, breeches and boots of a woodcutter.

A Devoted Wife

In spite of his strange life and his poverty, Israel married a fine young woman who was the daughter of a well-known rabbi. Hannah the daughter of Ephraim must have seen in her bridegroom the fine character and wonderful soul that others recognized later.

The story that was told years afterwards

A view of the town of Miedziboz, where the Baal Shem lived.

143

about their marriage is this. When Rabbi Ephraim first saw the young teacher, he was startled, for shining from Israel's forehead was a curved sign exactly like that he had seen for an instant on the little forehead of his own daughter, the first time he had seen her after she was born. This told him that his daughter and Israel ben Eliezer were bound to each other.

Rabbi Ephraim spoke to Israel and agreed that he should marry Hannah. But immediately after that, the older man fell ill and died. His son, Rabbi Gershon, found among his papers a marriage contract with a man he had never heard of.

"Hannah," Rabbi Gershon asked his sister "do you know this man Israel ben Eliezer?"

"No," said Hannah, "but if our father thought he was the man I should marry, I will do as he wished."

When Israel came to find his wife, the story continues, he was dressed like a poor farmer and spoke like an ignorant man. But Hannah said, "If my father has commanded this, it is God's command."

Hannah married Israel, believing that he must be a *Tzaddik,* a truly righteous man. It took much longer for her brother Gershon to realize that there was something remarkable about Israel ben Eliezer.

The couple left town and lived for some years in the mountains. Hannah helped him build a small hut. Two or three times a week she would help him load their wagon with clay or with firewood. Then this devoted wife would take his wagon into town, sell their poor wares, and buy flour for bread.

Eventually, his brother-in-law, Rabbi Gershon, helped them out of their poverty by buying them a tavern, so Israel could be an innkeeper. Israel was a kind host to all travelers; but Hannah did most of the work of keeping the inn, while her husband spent many hours thinking and praying by himself

The synagogue of the Baal Shem, interior view.

in the woods.

The Baal Shem

Soon the people who lived round about started to come to Israel with their problems. He was often able to help the sick with remedies he had learned in the mountains. More important was his ability to help those who were sick at heart. He became known for his wisdom and the good advice he was able to give. To those who were afflicted with sorrow, his wonderful faith in God brought new hope and joy.

Israel ben Eliezer became known as the *Baal Shem Tov,* Master of the Good Name. Soon he had followers who ate with him, prayed with him, and tried to learn from him how to live a good and happy life, trusting in God and rejoicing in His love.

The Besht—so called from the first letters of Baal Shem Tov—traveled about, talking to Jews in the small towns and telling them that they were all holy and all beloved in the eyes of God. He said that a man did not have to be a scholar, or wealthy, or a saint, in order to deserve this love.

God loved everyone, the least important man and even the sinner. "No man has sunk so low as to be unable to raise himself to God," said the Baal Shem. All could purify their

144

hearts and feel the joy of being loved by their Creator. In turn, man should delight in loving and serving God.

The Hasidim

The followers of the Baal Shem were called Hasidim, or Pious Ones. They would pray with great enthusiasm, even dancing with joy to show their devotion to God with all their heart and soul.

A traveler observing the Hasidim dancing and swaying as they prayed could not understand why they were doing so.

To explain it to him, the Baal Shem told a story. "Once," he said, "the guests at a feast were enjoying the happy music being played by a band of musicians. Soon they began dancing in time to the music.

"A deaf man passed by and looked in the window. He, poor man, could not hear the music. 'Such foolishness!' he exclaimed, 'for grown men to leap about for no reason.' "

The traveler understood. The music the Hasidim danced to was in their hearts, but to them it was very real. The traveler was deaf to this music, because he did not have the sincerity of heart of the Hasidim.

Another story told by the Hasidim shows how they felt about prayer:

An ignorant farmer, who lived far from the town, had a slow-witted son who never learned to read. The boy used to watch the sheep, and when he wanted to call them, he would whistle.

One Yom Kippur, the father took the boy to services in the town. The son could not read a word and knew no prayers. He watched the worshipers singing and praying, and wished he could join them. The final prayer was being said, asking God's forgiveness before the gates of Heaven closed.

"Father," asked the boy, "may I whistle?"

"Don't dare to whistle in the synagogue!" said the father.

But the boy's heart was moved. He wanted to express his love for God. The only way he could

show how he felt was to whistle. To his father's horror and the surprise of the congregation, he sent forth a piercing whistle louder than all the sounds of prayer in the synagogue.

At that moment, the Baal Shem turned and addressed the congregation. "None of your many prayers was sincere enough to ascend to God. But this whistle by the young shepherd boy, because it was uttered with true love of God, opened the gates of heaven so that all your prayers might be accepted."

It was the feeling behind the prayer that was of most importance to the Hasidim. They used a prayer book that was arranged by Isaac Luria, a teacher of Kabbalah. In their desire for prayer from the heart, they would not pray until they were sure they had reached the proper state of mind, the true feeling of devotion. They developed certain customs of their own, such as wearing white robes on Sabbath and holidays, to remind themselves of the purity with which one should keep the commandments.

Thousands of Jews became Hasidim, sharing the joy and enthusiasm of the Baal Shem's followers. They listened to every word of the Baal Shem and obeyed everything he said. He was their leader, the Tzaddik, or Righteous One, whom they addressed as Rebbe. He was the example of holy living that inspired them to a more noble life.

Parables of the Baal Shem

The Baal Shem never wrote any books. But his followers remembered and repeated his words, so they were not forgotten. Many of his lessons to them were told in the form of parables, or little stories with great meaning.

A Hasid asked the Baal Shem how he should act and dress in order to show humility, for it is said, "Walk humbly with thy God." To him the Baal Shem said, "A king was told that a man of humility would be rewarded. He dressed himself in old garments, moved from his palace to a small hut, and bowed before everyone. But when he looked into his true feelings, the king realized that he was very proud of all that he was doing. He was less humble than ever before. His adviser then said to him, 'Dress like a king; live like a king; allow the people to show respect to you; but be humble in your inmost heart.' "

The Baal Shem believed that everyone should be happy with whatever he had. Others, however, asked him why pious men so often are poorer than those who never pray at all. In reply he told this story: "A king wanted to please his loyal servants and said that to each one he would give his particular wish. Some asked for wealth, others for honor, others for comforts; and they were given these things.

"The most faithful servant of all said, 'My wish is to be allowed to spend time with the king, to enter and speak to him three times a day.' We who pray prefer being able to come close to God three times a day above all honors and wealth, and God grants us our wish."

Of the importance of the Tzaddik and the importance of every Hasid, the Baal Shem told this parable: "A rare and beautiful bird flew past the king's palace and lighted on the top of a tall tree. The king wanted to catch the bird and instructed his servants to form a human ladder, one standing on the shoulders of the other, until the highest one could cast a net over the bird. One man weakened and gave way, and all the others fell. Because of one man's weakness, the king could not get his desire.

"It is the same with us. The holy man depends on the support of men below him, and he in turn depends on even lower men in order that at least the Tzaddik might reach the top level of holiness and bring down God's love. But when one person fails, everyone falls, and the Tzaddik must begin trying again."

The synagogue of the Baal Shem.

After the Baal Shem

After the death of the Baal Shem, there arose many Hasidic leaders. Each town might have a Rebbe, and those of one town would consider their Rebbe to be greater than the leader of another town. In many cases, the son of the Rebbe would take over the position of honor after him, just the way a prince would follow his father, the king.

The most learned of the rabbis of the time opposed Hasidism, saying that it discouraged study of Torah. Hasidim, they said, forsook learning and broke with authority, keeping their own customs and showing too much reverence for their Rebbes.

In some Jewish communities, particularly in Lithuania, very few became Hasidim. In a large part of the Jewish world, the Hasidic movement grew and flourished. Hasidim to this day follow their Rebbes in communities in America, Europe and Israel. An outstanding group, called the *Lubavitcher Hasidim,* follow the teachings of Shneur Zalman, a Hasidic leader who emphasized study. He said wisdom, understanding and knowledge are the way to a good life.

The songs and the legends and teachings of the Hasidim have become a beloved part of the Jewish heritage.

The Hasidim have never tired of telling wonderful things about the Baal Shem. They tell how his father, Eliezer, was separated from his wife, captured and sold as a slave, and finally, still keeping his faith, found his way home. On the way he was met by Elijah the prophet, who told him, "Because of your piety and faith, you will have a son who will lighten the eyes of all Israel. Israel shall be his name, because in him shall be fulfilled the sentence of Isaiah: 'Thou art my servant, O Israel, in whom I will be glorified.' "

The Hasidim tell further that when Eliezer knew he was dying, he took the boy in his arms and said: "I see that you will make my light shine out. I am not to be allowed to rear you to manhood. But, dear son, remember all your days that God is with you, and that because of this, you need fear nothing in the world." Thus the Baal Shem grew up calm and strong in his faith, afraid of nothing.

The Baal Shem brought to his followers great gifts. He taught them that love of God means joy and fulfillment. He showed them the holiness in nature and in themselves, teaching them, "Everything created by God contains a spark of holiness. Serve the Lord in all things, even the smallest."

Said the Baal Shem, "Whoever lives in joy does his Creator's will. It is the goal of my whole life on earth to show my brethren, by living example, how one may serve God with merriment and rejoicing.

"For he who is full of joy is full of love for men and all fellow creatures."

Hasidim dancing in celebration of Simhat Torah.

SAYINGS OF THE BAAL SHEM

It shocks me to think that some men believe it is pleasing to God if they fast and make themselves suffer. Such dangerous things must not be done, for they show only melancholy and sadness. The glory of God shines not where there is mourning, but where there is joy in His law. The strength a man would be willing to lose through fasting, he should give to Torah and to prayer.

*   *   *

When you eat and take pleasure in the taste and sweetness of the food, remember that it is the Lord who has made the food sweet. You will, then, be serving Him by your eating.

*   *   *

Loving your fellowman as yourself means treating him as well as you treat yourself. Since you always find excuses for yourself when you do anything wrong, make excuses also for your fellowman.

*   *   *

One who sees faults in another and dislikes him for them surely has some of those same faults himself. The pure and good man can see only the goodness in others.

*   *   *

Do not think you are better than your fellow man. If his mind is not equal to yours, he is equal to you if he serves God as well as he can. A worm may be as important as you in the eyes of God, since it serves Him with all the strength He has given to it.

*   *   *

Do not keep thinking and worrying about your sins, for this prevents sincere service to God. Be sure you are sorry for what you have done, and resolve not to repeat it. Then serve God with joy.

*   *   *

Keep in mind always the knowledge that all good and pleasing things come from God. Every enjoyment then will become an act of praise to God, and a way of serving Him.

Elijah, Gaon of Vilna

1720 - 1797

If a visitor from out-of-town comes to your city, what do you like to show him? Would you take him to see a particular building, a museum, a university, a beautiful park, a waterfall?

When a visitor came to the city of Vilna, in Lithuania, two hundred years ago, any of the Vilna Jews would have known what to show him. The greatest boast of that community was not a mighty building or a wonder of nature, but a man.

The man was Elijah ben Solomon. He did not hold any official position. He was not the rabbi of Vilna, for he had refused to accept that title. He was not the head of a great *Yeshiva,* or school; nor was he by any means a man of great wealth.

All his life he lived quietly, not wanting to become a leader, too modest to give advice to others except when it was demanded of him.

Yet this was the man who was the crown of East European Jewry. He was called Elijah Gaon, the old title we remember from Babylonian times, meaning Excellency or Glory. He was the Gaon of Vilna, the pride and glory of Vilna.

The Family He Came From

The fame of Elijah of Vilna began early. When he was only seven years old, he gave a long speech on a Talmudic subject in the main synagogue of Vilna. But his family was well-known even before he was born. His ancestors were known for their modesty and goodness as well as their learning.

A great-grandfather of Elijah, Rabbi Moses, was known as Moshe Kraemer, or Moses the Shopkeeper. He made a living from a small store, where his wife waited on the customers, leaving him free to study.

Moshe Kraemer became Chief Rabbi of Vilna, but refused to accept any money from the community. His wife continued to keep the store. Somehow, business seemed to get better and better.

"How do you have so much left over at the end of the week?" the rabbi asked his wife. "Haven't you bought all the food for the Sabbath yet?"

"I have bought the food, but business has been very good. Every day more customers seem to come. Now we have extra money at the end of the week."

Rabbi Moshe was shocked to realize what had happened. "This must not be," he told his wife. "Customers are coming to the store out of respect for me, because I am the Chief Rabbi. It would be a sin for me to profit because of that.

"Besides, if we do more business, other shopkeepers must do less. This is taking the bread out of their mouths. I ask you, as soon as you have enough money each week for us to buy food and clothing, to close the shop."

His wife did so, willingly.

The son of Rabbi Moshe was Rabbi Elijah, who was so good to others and asked so little for himself that he was called Elijah the Saint. The same name was often given to Elijah's grandson, also called Elijah, the one of whom we now tell.

The Young Prodigy

Elijah the grandson was said, as a child, to be beautiful as well as brilliant. The beauty of his mind and soul shone through his face.

As an infant, Elijah began studying with his learned father, Rabbi Solomon. The father knew at once, as did all others who spoke to the boy, that he was a child prodigy. He was called the *Ilui,* the genius.

To have such a child was considered the greatest possible gift of God. The boy gave great joy to his parents, as well as to all the Jews of Vilna. By the age of ten, the young Ilui had received such a good start from his teachers that he could continue his studies by himself. A large congregation considered it a

A view of the city of Vilna. Vilna was called "The Jerusalem of Lithuania" because of the high standards of Jewish life and learning in that community.

blessing to hear him when he spoke as a child in the Vilna synagogue.

Elijah did not go to any of the well-known Yeshivot-schools of higher learning. He did not sit and listen to older teachers discussing the Talmud. By the time he was *Bar Mitzvah,* he had gone through the entire Talmud and much of the commentary by himself.

He did not stop there. In those days, most brilliant young Jewish students studied nothing else but the Talmud. The rabbis taught that everything worthwhile for a Jew to know could be found in the Talmud, and that reading "outside books," books on other subjects, was only a waste of time.

Elijah, in his solitary studies, learned much that he would not have learned at a Yeshiva. He studied the Bible more thoroughly than others did, learning its grammar and gaining a fine command of Hebrew. He studied as-

tronomy, the science of the universe, and anatomy, the science of the human body.

"Are these proper studies for a good pious Jew?" a friend of his father's once asked.

"If you consider Samuel of Nehardea, or Moses Maimonides, good examples of pious Jewish scholars," answered Rabbi Solomon, "then my son is doing the right thing; for the first was an astronomer, and the second a physician."

When Elijah had students of his own, there was one who had a good knowledge of languages, including Hebrew. "What can I do with this ability in language," asked the student, "to help Jewish learning?"

"What you can do," answered the Gaon, "is translate the writings of Euclid into Hebrew."

"But Reb Elijah," protested the student, "what kind of study is geometry for Jews?"

"Mathematics did not hurt Saadia Gaon. I wish that all the students of our Yeshivot might learn the science of numbers and logical thinking. From the writings of Euclid, they may learn to think clearly and organize their thoughts as Saadia did."

A New Way of Study

For centuries, the learned Jews of every country had studied the Talmud over and over. Many commentaries had been written on each sentence. The students considered every commentary to be true. If there seemed to be disagreement they would use their keen minds to find a way to explain the difference. This method of clever, involved discussion was called *pilpul.*

Elijah of Vilna did not use the method of pilpul. He wanted to understand the Talmud for what it really was, to go back to the original text and to see what the rabbis had actually meant.

He and a student might be considering a passage in the Talmud where an extra, unnecessary word seemed to be inserted. The student might say that one commentator gave this special reason for the odd word, and another gave a different reason, but that he had found a way to explain both.

The Vilna Gaon might then show the student a similar passage in another volume.

"This is the *Talmud Yerushalmi,*" he would tell the student. "You know that at the time that the *amoraim,* the great teachers in Babylonia, were discussing the *Mishnah,* the same thing was going on in the school of Palestine. The Jerusalem Talmud has almost the same passage as our Babylonian Talmud. But you will notice that the extra word appears in the next sentence, where it belongs and makes very good sense.

"This is the simple explanation. The word is in the wrong place in our editions of the Talmud because some copyist or editor made a mistake, perhaps a thousand years ago. It is a common human error, and all the explanations of the commentators were unnecessary."

Elijah was able to show that some sentences were hard to understand because of some small mistake in a word or even one letter. Others seemed strange because they contained a Greek word, or a scientific term which the rabbis of old understood, but which had fallen out of use.

There is a saying in the Talmud that a man should spend the first forty years of his life studying, gathering knowledge; and the next forty years teaching, or giving out knowledge.

Elijah Gaon wanted to follow this suggestion, and did so almost exactly. He started to teach and write when he was forty. The number of books that the Gaon of Vilna wrote is hard to believe. There were more than seventy volumes. Some of them have never been copied or printed. He wrote commentaries on almost every great book of Jewish tradition, including many works of *Kabbalah.*

Fame Comes to Him Who Flees It

Elijah of Vilna was a modest man who never wanted fame. He would not become rabbi of Vilna. He prayed in a small synagogue, that became a model for others because he left

עליות אליהו

תולדות האדם הגדול בענקים

אלופנו גאון הגאונים, וחסיד כאחד מהראשונים, נכנס לפני ולפנים ופתח גנזי מטמונים, וחכמות וסרטים שונים, סביב לרגלו חונים ראש גולת אריאל, כשם אליהו גאון וחסיד מווילנא, נודע בישראל

נאספו רועי הקדרים, גדולי הדור הנודעים בשערים, והעריכו לזה מאמרים ולראשונה יבואו דברים נפלאים, חכמה ודעת קרושים סלאים, נקראים בשם

עלית השער
הכלית יסוד החיבור

מעלות הסולם
דרך הגאון והילוכו בקורש

עלית קיר
ע"ד חיבוריו וכתביו

A page of one of the many learned works about the Vilna Gaon.

152

out certain long and difficult prayers, and encouraged singing by the whole congregation.

Even when people asked his advice, he was unwilling to give it. "Why should my words have any effect," he once asked, "when I am a younger man than the one who is asking?" Yet from the time he was still in his teens, old and learned Jews came to him with questions.

Not only did he not ask for honor. He did not even ask for what was really his own.

It happened once that for a period of years the man who was in charge of giving Elijah a certain amount of money each month began to take some of the money for himself.

"Please buy less food," Elijah told his wife. "From now on, I want no more than one meal a day."

By his eating less, he and his family managed to get along on the smaller amount of money. Because he did not want to accuse a fellow man of stealing, he went hungry himself; until some one else found out about the situation.

The Gaon Speaks Out

There were times, however, when Elijah's devotion to Jewish ideals made him speak out strongly.

The Board of Jewish Charities in Vilna met one day to discuss a bothersome problem.

"Why should we good householders be exposed to the annoyance of beggars coming to our doors?" asked a leading citizen. "Let the poor go to a central office, where an official will consider their requests."

"A good idea," agreed the wealthier members.

"But let us first ask Reb Elijah his opinion," said one.

A delegation went to the Gaon, where he sat alone in his small back room studying.

"Reb Elijah, we have come to ask you if you approve of our new policy," came the request.

"What new policy?" asked the Gaon. "I have heard only of an old policy, a very old one."

"What do you mean?" asked the members of the Board.

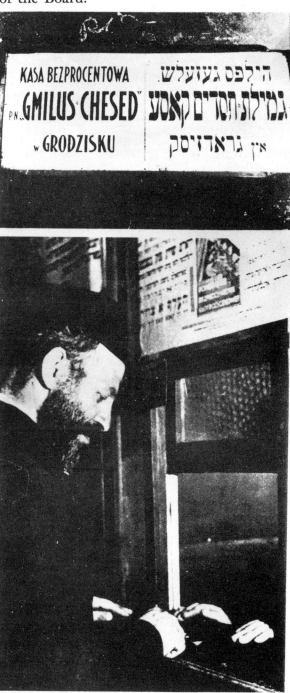

The tradition of G'milut Hasadim (free loans) is an ancient and honorable one. G'milut Hesed means "doing kindness."

"It is a policy as old as Sodom, the biblical city that was destroyed by God because of its wickedness in the time of Abraham our father," said the Gaon. "In that evil city, poor men were also forbidden to ask the householders for help."

The good citizens understood and were ashamed. They changed the law. From that time on they also gave the Gaon a sum of money each year for him to give where it was needed, without making everyone who needed help announce it to the community.

They knew that no one would hesitate about going to the good, kind and honest Elijah Gaon for help.

Another change in Jewish life brought the Gaon of Vilna out of seclusion. When Hasidism began to gain followers in his part of the world, he announced that no Hasidic group or congregation should be allowed in Lithuania. He felt the Hasidic teaching made Jews follow superstition and forsake true learning.

The influence of this gentle, usually silent man was so great that he stopped Hasidism from growing in Lithuania and nearby areas.

Till his death when he was almost eighty, the Gaon of Vilna spent most of his hours in study. As a known writer, a brilliant teacher, a man whose Jewish knowledge was greater than that of any other living man, he continued to study every day of his life.

Mothers could pray that their children might live by his example. He was the great hero whom they were to copy. Every Jew, whatever his business, no matter how low or difficult his job, was inspired by the Vilna Gaon to take some time for study every day. Early in the morning before going to their hard day's work, or between afternoon and evening prayers, the humblest Jews would devote some precious hours to study.

A student once spoke to the Vilna Gaon of his love of learning. "Wouldn't it be the fulfillment of your dearest wish," he asked, "if by a miracle an angel would touch you and cause you to know all that there is to know?"

"No," said the Gaon. "If an angel were to reveal to me all the mysteries of the Torah, it would please me little, for study is more important than knowledge. Only what man achieves through effort is dear to him."

In a lifetime of devoted and joyous study, the Vilna Gaon indeed showed what was dearest to him, and what should be dear to the Jewish people: the love and pursuit of learning, the study of a rich and glorious tradition.

SAYINGS OF THE GAON OF VILNA

A child should begin study with the Bible, and learn it well, so that he knows its language and grammar as well as its contents; then he can go on to the six divisions of the Mishnah, with the important commentaries; and finally, when he is prepared for it, to the Talmud in general.

* * *

When you lead your sons and daughters in the good way, let your words be kind and gentle, for the only true discipline or obedience is that which is won from the willing heart.

* * *

Treat all men with courtesy, pleasantness and respect.

* * *

A Jewish scholar must learn all the seven branches of knowledge. A knowledge of all the sciences, algebra, geometry, astronomy, music, etc., is necessary to understand the Torah, for they are all included in it. If a man is lacking in general knowledge, he will be lacking a hundred times as much in the knowledge of the Torah, for Torah and science go together.

* * *

We cannot and should not disregard or fight our desires; but we can and must purify them and direct them to worthy goals.

* * *

I do not spend time thinking about the reward that may come for doing good deeds. Elijah can serve God without the promise of a World to Come.

* * *

It may be proper to call me an observant Jew, but as to being a saint, as I have been told they call me, I have not reached that stage yet.

Moses Mendelssohn

1729 - 1786

In a drizzling October rain, as darkness was beginning to fall, a small, stooped figure approached the gates of the great city of Berlin. The traveler, who had come a long way on foot, was a fourteen-year-old boy. He had long since finished the bread his mother had given him for the journey; now all he carried were a small bundle of Sabbath clothes, and the quill pen and ink-bottle that his father had given him.

At the gate, the boy stopped, and knocked gently. No one answered. Again he knocked. The gate opened a small distance, and an angry face looked out.

"What do you want, getting me out into the rain?" asked the watchman.

"Please, sir," said the young traveler, "I want to be admitted to Berlin."

The watchman's face turned red. From the way the boy pronounced the German words, he could tell a good deal about him.

"We don't need any more Jews here!" shouted the man. "Especially not cripples and beggars. Go back to whatever little town you came from."

"I am not a beggar," said the boy softly. "I am a student." The words of the watchman hurt him deeply, for he was a hunchback as a result of a childhood disease he had suffered.

"What kind of student? From what school?" sneered the watchman.

"I am a student from Dessau," said the boy. "I have followed my teacher, Rabbi David Frankel. I want to study Talmud with him."

"And that's all?" asked the man suspiciously.

"That's all I want in the world," said the young man. "All I want is to study and learn."

"All right," said the ruffian. "Come in and go straight to your rabbi's house. But remember, you can stay only as long as you don't make a nuisance of yourself to our good citizens."

This was the welcome young Moses Mendelssohn received when he first came to Berlin. Years later, when he died, kings and princes mourned for him.

Self-education

What was so remarkable about Moses of Dessau? He was very far from handsome in face or form. He never studied at a university, not even at a high school. The Germans of his time, considering the Jews an inferior people, kept them in certain towns only, giving passes to a few to live in the large cities. They believed it right to keep them out of schools, to prevent them from getting jobs or owning land.

The Jews themselves lived in their own groups as best they could. They studied their own tradition and had no hope of entering the outside world. Thus the young Moses came to Berlin speaking a poor, broken German, and without even a last name. As the son of Menahem Mendel, he took the name of Mendelssohn.

All young Moses Mendelssohn owned was a brilliant mind and a love for learning. Helped by Rabbi Frankel, he found books and sought out scholars. He taught himself correct German, sciences, and all the other things he might have learned at a German university.

He worked as a *sofer,* a scribe or writer of Hebrew manuscripts, for he had learned this skill from his father. When he was twenty-one he became a tutor for the children of one of the few wealthy Jewish families that were allowed by the emperor Frederick the Great to live in Berlin.

The young Moses was happy because he was learning. But all about him he saw that his people were despised. If occasionally Moses might meet and talk with a German professor, the professor would always be amazed to find a Jew who could talk perfect

German and discuss things of the mind.

The Playwright Lessing

The young scholar heard of a play called *The Jews*. With some misgivings, he bought a copy and read it. To his surprise and delight, the playwright showed in the script that Jews were not hateful people, but could be noble and kind.

"Have you ever met Gotthold Lessing, the playwright?" Moses asked Rabbi Frankel. "No," said the rabbi. "How should a leading writer of Germany associate with Jews?"

Moses Mendelssohn sometimes turned his active mind to something besides study. He was an expert chess player. One man with whom he enjoyed playing was Aaron Gumperz, an older scholar.

One day, after losing a game to Moses, Aaron said to him, "I have a better chess partner for you."

The next day, Aaron Gumperz lost a game to none other than Gotthold Lessing, whom he had known for some time. To him he said the same thing: "I have a better chess partner for you."

"Bring him on," said the great Lessing.

We have never learned which player won the first match, but both won something more valuable. The two fine souls became bound in a bond of friendship.

As a friend of Lessing's, Moses Mendelssohn was able to meet more and more of the intelligent thinkers and writers of Berlin. One of Lessing's fellow-writers, after meeting Mendelssohn, admitted, "You know, Lessing, I must confess that when your play *The Jews* came out, I was one of those who thought you had gone out of your mind. It seemed so ridiculous to show Jews as decent people like us. But now that I have met your friend, I can believe your point."

Moses Mendelssohn had been writing down many of his thoughts in the form of little essays. When he told Lessing, the playwright insisted that he must see them.

Mendelssohn gave him a sheaf of papers, which Lessing took home, promising to read them immediately.

The next time Mendelssohn met him, he asked, "What did you think of my essays?"

"I'm sorry. I haven't had time to read them properly," said Lessing.

A week later, Mendelssohn asked again. "Perhaps you can return my essays to me?"

"I've lent them to a friend," said Lessing.

Mendelssohn was always considerate. He didn't want to bother his friend. But he had no other copies of his essays, and he wanted them back. Finally he asked again.

"I'll have them for you tomorrow," said Lessing.

The next day he handed Mendelssohn a little book. It was nicely printed and bound. Its title was *Philosophical Conversations,* and the author's name, printed on the cover, was Moses Mendelssohn.

The young man, who had not even learned to speak German correctly till he was almost grown, found himself to be a much-admired philosopher and writer in the German language.

Mendelssohn Becomes Famous

Moses Mendelssohn began to write articles for German magazines. The leading professors, artists and writers of Germany wanted to meet him and talk to him, to sound out his brilliant mind and hear his opinions.

As a critic for a magazine, Mendelssohn once wrote an article criticizing some poems written by the emperor, Frederick the Great.

There is a story that Frederick, angry at this criticism, sent for the writer to punish him.

Mendelssohn spoke softly to the emperor. He spoke not of poetry, but of bowling, or, as they called it, playing at ninepins.

"As the emperor, you should be respected," said Mendelssohn. "But anybody who chooses to write poetry is like someone who plays at ninepins. Whoever takes his chances at ninepins, whether he is king or peasant, must allow the pinboy to tell him his score."

The emperor was pleased at the clever answer, and had to admit it was a fair one. If he joined the game of writing verses, he had to obey the same rules as other poets.

Mendelssohn remained modest. He knew his shortcomings, and never forgot his ugly appearance. He did not expect a beautiful or wealthy girl to want to marry him. He was over thirty when he proposed to a plain Jewish girl from his hometown, named Fromet Guggenheim. She saw the beauty of his mind and soul, and accepted the proposal.

Their household was a fine and happy one, in which six brilliant and talented children grew up.

Soon after he was married, Mendelssohn entered a contest. The Berlin Academy of Sciences asked for essays on philosophy. There were to be no names, only a code name, on the essays when the judges read them, so that they would be sure to judge fairly.

The prize entry was chosen, with two runners-up. Then the judges looked for the names of the authors.

One name they recognized immediately. The second-prize essay had been written by the greatest philosopher and most revered thinker of Germany, Immanuel Kant.

The first prize had been awarded to Moses Mendelssohn.

With this new honor, Mendelssohn's fame spread far and wide. Yet he still was treated, like other Jews, as an inferior person. He had to have special permission to stay in Berlin, and there were places and institutions he was not allowed to enter. He could have been forced to leave the city at any time; he could

have been put in jail for no cause, without any **defense.**

Appeals were made to Frederick the Great and finally Mendelssohn was given a rare privilege. He was given special status, so that all the laws against Jews and the special taxes they had to pay no longer applied to him. He was accepted almost as a citizen of Prussia.

His Ideas on Religion

Many Christian friends of Mendelssohn were unsure about their own religion. They asked him his opinion about the soul of man. They especially wanted to know if scientific thinking, or reason, could prove that the soul lived on after death.

Mendelssohn wrote a little book that taught that the soul of man is immortal, that it cannot be completely lost or destroyed. A Christian teacher said to him, "As I have studied more and more, I have been losing faith in God. I have been questioning whether God really cares about every human soul; whether my own life is of any importance. You, Mendelssohn, have given me new faith. Now I believe and am happy."

Mendelssohn was sometimes called the German Plato or the German Socrates, after the two great Greek philosophers of ancient times. They even said he looked like Socrates, who was supposed to have been a very ugly

Graveyard of the Dessau community showing the tombstone of Mendelssohn's father to the right.

man.

The friendship Mendelssohn had with so many Christian leaders led to some trouble. A Swiss preacher admired Mendelssohn very much. He published a book about Christianity, with an introduction asking Mendelssohn to read it and leave his Jewish faith.

Mendelssohn never wanted to join a public argument. He did not want to offend anyone. But he had to answer. He wrote a reply, saying he was convinced of his own religion, Judaism, and would not leave it. He said he respected all religions that taught their members to be good.

He spoke of freedom of religion for all groups, telling that Jews do not try to convert others, since they believe all good people are pleasing to God. He quoted the statement of the Rabbis: "The righteous of the nations of the world have a share in the world-to-come."

The preacher apologized to Moses Mendelssohn. Many others were interested in the Jewish point of view. The devotion of the famous philosopher to his own religion impressed them, while he had spoken so gently that no Christian could feel insulted.

Mendelssohn Helps His People

Mendelssohn had long been an admirer of Moses Maimonides. In many writings, particularly a book called *Jerusalem,* he tried to help his people understand their religion better, as Maimonides had done in his time with the "Guide for the Perplexed."

He made sure to tell the Jews that they must keep the laws of Torah and Talmud as well as the general laws of humanity. Even though Jews may have different ideas about God and the universe, they must in all their deeds obey Jewish law. They are to be judged by their actions and their way of life, rather than their beliefs.

Jews of many countries looked to Mendelssohn for help and advice. "He is a friend of the emperor," they said. "He can help where no one else can."

Indeed Mendelssohn devoted himself to improving the lot of his people. He did his best to change the laws that kept the Jews in fear and separated them from all other groups in the lands in which they lived.

"The greatest need," he told Lessing, "is for education. They must be able to speak good German and they must learn the subjects that make a man of culture. Then they will fit in with the society around them."

"How can you help them?" asked Lessing. "You cannot expect them to be admitted to the universities; and they cannot even read what you write, if they don't know German."

"I will translate the Bible into German for them," said Mendelssohn. "They all know it in Hebrew. In reading this translation, they will learn German."

Mendelssohn's work helped to free his people from some of the laws and taxes that had made their lives difficult. His example encouraged young Jews to study modern subjects and find their place in the world. Eventually some of them were admitted to the universities.

His mind and character showed the Christian world that a Jew could be the finest type of person. He was considered the noblest citizen of Berlin, and was praised as the greatest master of the language. "Appreciate the beauty of our language," he advised the writers of his day, "and do not try to copy the styles of other countries."

Gotthold Lessing wrote another play, called *Nathan the Wise.* Nathan in the play is a wise, kind and honorable Jew, living in Palestine at the time of the Crusades. His whole family having been killed by Crusaders, he has raised an orphaned Christian girl as his own.

A Christian knight saves her life when she is eighteen. The knight thinks that all Jews are bad, but both he and the Moslem ruler learn how good a Jew can be when they get to know Nathan. The knight at first thinks he cannot marry the girl, Recha, because she is a Jew. He finds out she is a Christian by birth; but, further, the Moslem ruler finds that his enemy, the Christian knight, is really his long-lost nephew.

In all this involved plot, the message comes through: persons of all religions can be good, and can live together in peace.

There was much excitement about the play. No one could object, this time, because Lessing had presented a Jew as a noble character. They knew that the model for Nathan the Wise was Moses Mendelssohn.

At Mendelssohn's death, he was mourned not only by his own good wife and children; not only by the Jews of Europe, who looked to him to plead with princes in their behalf. He was mourned by the leaders and rulers of Prussia and the other German-speaking states. He had brought new beauty to the German language and new light to German thought.

Forty years before, the hunch-backed boy had waited at a closed door. He had almost been turned away from the gates of Berlin. Now he was mourned as the most important citizen and the best mind of the country.

He had not only opened the gates of Berlin for himself. He had also opened the door to citizenship and civil rights for the Jews of his time.

With Mendelssohn, the Jews entered the modern world.

A page from the Book of Ruth of the Bible, with the Mendelssohn translation and explanation in the upper left column. It is in German, printed in Hebrew letters.

SELECTIONS FROM MOSES MENDELSSOHN

It is interesting to see how prejudice against the Jews has changed. In times past we were accused of sacrilege against holy things, and they made every effort to convert us to Christianity. Now they accuse us of superstition, ignorance, bad manners, and lack of service to the state. They keep us from schools and employment; they block the road of improvement for us, and then reprove us because we lack education or skill. They tie our hands, and then reproach us for doing nothing.

*   *   *

As I see it, the Jews do not have a revealed religion, but a revealed law. They have laws, commands, instructions, which teach them how to conduct themselves, but there are no dogmas. There is not in the Torah a single command, "Thou shalt believe" or "not believe."

*   *   *

The written and oral laws which form our religion are binding on the Jewish people only. All the other nations of the earth, we believe, must obey only the natural laws of decency and justice. Those who regulate their lives according to these laws are called "the righteous of the nations of the earth," and are worthy in the eyes of God. Since, according to the Rabbis, the just and virtuous men of every nation deserve salvation as much as the most observant Jew, we do not try to make converts to Judaism.

*   *   *

Be good citizens and devote yourselves to the land in which you have settled, but remain faithful to the religion of your fathers.

*   *   *

If citizenship cannot be obtained in any other way than by giving up our Law, we are very sorry, but we must give up citizenship.

*   *   *

All the nations of the world seem to have been afflicted with this madness, believing that religion can be established by a rule of iron, that the teaching of salvation can be spread only by persecution, and that God, who is Love, can be brought to mankind by hate. Give thanks to God that this madness is disappearing from the earth. The nations are learning to bear with one another, and are beginning to show signs of love and mercy toward you too, which in time may fill the hearts of men with true brotherly affection. Oh, my brothers, follow the example of love; show respect and tolerance among yourselves. Love, and you will be loved.

GLOSSARY

Below are some words which you may have met for the first time in your reading of *Heroes of Jewish Thought*.

AMIDAH (Hebrew: "standing")
The central prayer in every Jewish service, recited in a low tone as the congregation stands. It is often repeated by the cantor. Because it originally contained eighteen blessings, it is also called the *Shemoneh Esreh*, meaning "eighteen." The blessings include praise for God, thanks for His gifts, and petitions for the future, ending with the prayer for peace.

AMORA (plural AMORAIM)
One who speaks or explains, the name given to the interpreters of the Mishnah in the schools of Palestine and of Babylonia. More than 3000 of these scholars are known by name. Their work, continued from about the year 200 to the year 500, resulted in the Gemara.

ARAMAIC
A language similar to Hebrew, spoken in Babylonia and the entire Near East. From the time of the first Exile (586 B.C.E.) the Jews spoke and wrote Aramaic as well as Hebrew, and it was the common language of Palestine in Talmudic times. A small part of the Bible, the entire Gemara, the Zohar, and such prayers as the *Kaddish* and *Kol Nidre* are in the Aramaic language.

ASHKENAZI (plural ASHKENAZIM)
Jews from Germany and from eastern Europe as distinguished from Jews of Spain and other countries around the Mediterranean Sea. The Ashkenazi pronunciation of Hebrew has been replaced in Israel by the Sephardi pronunciation.

BET DIN (Hebrew: "House of Judgment")
A court consisting of rabbis, which judges according to Jewish law. The Sanhedrin, with seventy-one members, was the highest *Bet Din;* the local courts were required to have three judges.

CODES
Organized lists of Jewish laws, based on the Torah and Talmud. Some codes mentioned in this book are the Mishneh Torah of Maimonides, the Turim of Jacob ben Asher, and the Shulhan Arukh of Joseph Caro.

DAYAN
A rabbi who is a judge of religious and civil matters for a Jewish community.

ESSENES

A Jewish group during the last years of the Second Temple, who lived in separate communities near the Dead Sea, avoided pleasure, and devoted themselves to study and writing.

EXILARCH

Leader of the Exile, or head of the Jewish community of Babylonia. He had much power over the people, appointing judges and collecting taxes; but the king or caliph of Babylonia had authority over him. In Hebrew his title was *Rosh Golah*, in Aramaic, *Resh Galuta;* both mean Head of the Exile.

GALUT

Hebrew word meaning Exile, referring to the forced scattering of Jews first to Babylonia and then throughout the world by action of their enemies. Another form of the word is *Golah*.

GAON (plural GEONIM)

Title of the head of the academy at Sura or Pumbedita, meaning "excellency" or "glory." These scholars of Babylonia led the study and explanation of the Talmud, and answered questions on Jewish law from all over the world.

GEMARA

Second and largest part of the Talmud, consisting of discussions on the first and basic part, the Mishnah. The Gemara is the work of the Amoraim (200 to 500 C.E.). It has been the major study of Jewish scholars for hundreds of years.

GHETTO

Special parts of cities in Italy and Germany where Jews were forced to live, during the Middle Ages and afterwards.

HASIDIM (singular HASID)

Members of the Hasidic movement founded by Israel Baal Shem Tov. They believe that purity of heart and joy in worship are the proper way to serve God. Many Hasidic leaders, called Tzaddikim, have taught love of God and love of fellowman to their devoted followers.

HEDER (Hebrew: "room")

Small school, often in the home of the teacher, where children would receive their elementary Jewish education.

KABBALAH (Hebrew: "tradition")

Jewish mystical teachings about God, the nature of the world, and man and his soul. The most important book of Kabbalah is the *Zohar*. Kabbalah was particularly studied by the scholars of Safed and by the Hasidim.

KAHAL

The organized Jewish community of towns in Germany and Poland, whose highest official was the rabbi.

KALLAH

Name given to the gatherings for study at the academies of Sura and Pumbedita in Babylonia, during the months of Elul and Adar. Students came from all parts of the country for these sessions, which were founded by Rav.

KARAITES

Jewish group which wanted to follow only the Written Law, the Bible, and rejected the Talmud and all the teachings of the rabbis. After the death of their first leader, Anan ben David, later leaders developed a Karaite interpretation of the Torah, differing in many ways from the Rabbanite, or traditional Jewish interpretation.

KASHRUT

Fulfilment of the Jewish laws of Bible and Talmud concerning the preparing and eating of food.

KHAZARS

A tribe that lived in what is now southern Russia, and in the late eighth century, under their king Bulan, converted to Judaism.

KIDDUSH

The prayer of sanctification, or "making holy," which is recited by the head of each household over a cup of wine at the beginning of each Sabbath or festival.

KIDDUSH HASHEM (Hebrew: "sanctification of God's name")

Any act which brings credit or glory to Jews and Judaism, often meaning the acceptance of a martyr's death.

KORAN

The holy book of Islam. It contains some stories and characters of the Bible and regards Abraham and Moses as prophets.

LADINO

The Jewish-Spanish dialect, written in Hebrew letters, spoken by Jews of the Mediterranean countries. Although it has some Hebrew words it is more like the Spanish language of the Middle Ages.

MARRANOS (Hebrew: Anusim)

Jews of Spain and Portugal who were forced to accept Christianity, but tried secretly to keep Jewish law. Those who were discovered were put to death. Many Marranos escaped to Turkey, Italy, Holland, and even to America.

MENORAH

The seven-branched candelabrum used in the Temple in Jerusalem. The name is often given to the Hanukkiah, the eight-branched candelabrum used on Hanukkah.

MESSIAH: (Hebrew: Mashiah, "anointed one")

A king or leader who will bring peace and justice to the world. The hope for a Messiah who would save them from their persecutors and bring them back to the land of Israel gave strength to the Jewish people through the centuries.

MIDRASH

A way of finding more meaning in the words of the Bible. The great books of Midrashim were collected in Palestine in Talmudic times. They contain legends, explanations, and lessons for daily life learned from the stories in the Bible.

MISHNAH

The great collection of laws and traditions put together by Judah Ha-Nasi and his school about the year 200. This edition of the Oral Law is organized into six "orders." It is the basic work of the Talmud.

MITZVAH (plural MITZVOT)

Word meaning "commandment," referring to the 613 laws contained in the Torah. A Jew who observes the laws can be called a *Shomer Mitzvot,* a "keeper of commandments." Mitzvah is also used to refer to a good deed, such as helping the poor. A Bar Mitzvah is one who is old enough to be responsible for keeping commandments.

MO'ED

Hebrew for festival. It is the name of the Second Order, or division, of the Mishnah, which deals with the Sabbath, festivals, and fast days.

NAGID

Hebrew for Prince. Title given in Moslem countries to heads of Jewish communities.

NASI

Hebrew for Prince or President. Title for the head of the Sanhedrin, later for the head of the leading school of Palestine and for the Patriarch recognized by the Roman rulers as leader of the Jews of the country. In later days the Nasi was always a descendant of Hillel. The best known was Judah Ha-Nasi.

PHARISEES (Hebrew PERUSHIM)

Teachers and religious leaders of the Jews in the time of the Second Temple. They stressed study of the Torah and of the Oral Law, trying to bring the people to righteous and holy living.

RABBI

Hebrew for "My master" or "My teacher." The title has been used for teachers of the law from Talmudic times. The meaning of the word shows that the rabbi is not a priest who prays for the people, but a learned man who guides and teaches them.

RABBANITE

Term used by the Karaites to denote those who followed the teachings of the rabbis.

REBBE

Yiddish form of the word rabbi, usually referring to a Hasidic rabbi.

RESPONSA (Hebrew "Teshuvot")

Latin word meaning "answers to questions." The Geonim of Babylonia wrote answers to questions on Jewish law sent to them from all over the world. Great rabbis of later generations, until the present day, have continued to write Responsa. Many collections of Responsa from different countries and different centuries have been printed. They help to show what the life of the Jews was like at various times.

SADDUCEES

The party of the priests and kings at the time of the Pharisees. The Sadducees were strict about the Law and stressed the Temple service.

SANHEDRIN

Talmudic term for a court of law, from the Greek word meaning "assembly." The Great Sanhedrin during the time of the Second Temple had seventy-one members; the lower court had twenty-three. Many rules for conducting trials in a fair and just way are described in the Talmud, in the section called Sanhedrin.

SEDER

The order of service and festive meal at home on the first evenings of the Passover holiday.

SEPHARDI (plural SEPHARDIM)

Name given to Jews of Spanish and Portuguese descent, including many who settled in Italy, Turkey, and all parts of the Middle East. Sephardic Jews migrated to Holland, England, and the Americas before Ashkenazi Jews.

SHABBAT

The Sabbath (a word taken from the Hebrew), the first day of weekly rest. It is one of the Ten Commandments and is our most important holiday. Yom Kippur, the Day of Atonement, is called Sabbath of Sabbaths, and is the only day that can be said to surpass the Sabbath in holiness.

SHAMMASH

The man in charge of the synagogue building and the order of services.

SHEMA (Hebrew: "Hear")

"Hear O Israel, the Lord our God, the Lord is One." This is the central statement of loyalty to Judaism. It is recited during evening and morning prayers, several times in shorter form during the day, and before going to sleep.

SIDDUR

The Jewish prayer book, containing prayers for every day and for the Sabbath. Prayers, psalms and poems have been added to the Siddur since the first one was put together about a thousand years ago.

SIMHAT TORAH (Hebrew: "Rejoicing of the Law")

The day ending the Sukkot holidays, when the reading of the Torah for the year is completed and the new reading is begun. It is a time of song and joy in the synagogue.

SOFER

A scribe, the skilled and pious man who writes by hand the scrolls of the Torah and other religious inscriptions.

TALMUD

The great collection of tradition and laws which, after the Bible itself, is the basis for the Jewish religion. It is composed of the Mishnah, the work of scholars from the end of Bible days to about 200 C.E.; and the Gemara, completed around the year 550. It thus records a thousand years of development and interpretation of Jewish law.

TALMUD BAVLI

The Babylonian Talmud, which includes the Gemara developed by the Amoraim of the Babylonian Jewish community, has been the center of Jewish study through the ages.

TALMUD YERUSHALMI

The Talmud of Palestine, with the shorter Gemara developed by the Palestinian schools, called "Jerusalem Talmud" although it was not produced in that city.

TANNA (plural TANNAIM)

Name given to teachers and scholars whose interpretations of Jewish law are recorded in the Mishnah.

TORAH

Translated as "Teaching" or "Law." It was originally applied to the first five books of the Bible, the books of Moses, which are written in every *Sefer Torah,* or scroll of the Torah. The term Torah however, is often used to mean all of Jewish religious tradition. The five books of Moses contain the Mitzvot, the commandments for Jewish living, and are therefore studied with great devotion and read in the synagogue throughout the year.

TOSAFOT

Additional commentaries on the Talmud written after the time of Rashi.

TZADDIK

A righteous man. In the Talmud it is said that 36 tzaddikim in each generation make the world worthy to survive. Hasidim often call their Rebbe by the name, Tzaddik.

YESHIVAH (plural YESHIVOT)

An academy where Talmud is studied and where students may be ordained as rabbis. The name was first used in Palestine at the time of Johanan ben Zakkai. It has been used in Babylonia, in all the countries of Europe, and in America and Israel today. An elementary school where children receive Jewish education may also be called a yeshivah.

YIDDISH

The Yiddish language was developed in the Middle Ages by the Jews in Germany. When these Jews moved to Poland and Lithuania, they carried their language with them. Though it is written in Hebrew script and contains many Hebrew words, Yiddish is basically German. It is, after Hebrew, the most widely used language of the Jewish people.

INDEX